J   Provost, Gary,
PRO   1944-

        David and Max

$12.95

DATE		

David and Max

David and Max

by Gary Provost and Gail Levine-Provost

THE JEWISH PUBLICATION SOCIETY
New York • Philadelphia • Jerusalem

Manufactured in the United States of America

Jacket illustration by Steffi Karen Rubin

The Jewish Publication Society
Philadelphia • New York • Jerusalem
5749–1988

Library of Congress Cataloging-in-Publication Data

Provost, Gary, 1944–
    David and Max / by Gary Provost and Gail Levine-Provost.—1st
ed.
    Summary: While spending the summer with his grandfather
Max and helping him search for a friend believed to have perished
in the Holocaust, twelve-year-old David discovers many things
about Max's terrible years during World War II and subsequent
family relationships
    ISBN 0-8276-0315-0
    [1. Grandfathers—Fiction.   2. Holocaust, Jewish (1939–1945)—
Fiction.]   I. Levine-Provost, Gail.   II. Title.
PZ7.P948Dav   1988
[Fic]—dc 19   88-6856
                                                                        CIP
                                                                        AC

For my brother, Steve.
And to the memory of my grandparents, Max and Clara Levine, and David and Anna Rubinstein; my aunts and uncle, Sylvia Needelman, Rose Weiser, and Mac Jennis; Sylvia Freidus; and my daughter, Marci.

—Gail

To the memory of my mother, Evelyn; my father, Red; and my brother, Billy.

—Gary

The authors would like to thank Larry Wilenker, who gave generously of his time, and shared with us his memories.

CHAPTER ONE

Most of the time I called my grandfather Max Levene. Some people might have thought it was disrespectful, but Grampa never did, and I never meant it to be.

He used to call me on the telephone and he'd say, "Hello, Duvid"—that's how he pronounced David—"this is Max Levene, your grandfather." I always thought that was the biggest riot. I mean, it wasn't as if I knew fifteen other guys named Max Levene. I liked to tease Max and I would say, "Levene? Levene? That does sound familiar," and Max would say, "Duvid, it's me, Max Levene, your grandfather. Me, Max Levene." We would go on like that for a while, until finally I'd admit that I knew it was Grampa all along. We had some great times, me and Max.

Now he was dead.

And I still hadn't cried.

I sat at the back of the small parlor, trembling as if I were terribly cold, but not crying. Nana, my grandmother, sat beside me. She was crying enough for the two of us. In fact, Nana was wailing like a wounded animal, and the pitiful sound she made must have echoed all through the funeral home, where hundreds of other people had come for Max Levene's funeral.

Well, David, I thought, the doctors were right. They had said Max would die soon from his weak heart. I had gone around telling people that doctors are crazy. "Hey, not Max Levene," I would say. "He's indestructible," and people would look at me with pity in their eyes, probably because they could tell I was scared. Anyhow, the doctors were right and I was wrong and now my grampa was there inside that long wooden box at the front of the room, lying quiet and still, like a thing instead of a person.

This small room was for close family members, so we could be alone with Max before we had to go and face all the second cousins and distant nephews and friends from the synagogue. And, of course, all the odd characters Max had known over the years. Max was like that. Nana would send him to the store for a quart of milk and he'd come home an hour later and say, "I met this very interesting man. Walberg's the name. He collects bathtubs."

My mother and father, my younger brother Markie, Nana, and I were all together in the little parlor, but I bet we all felt as if we were alone. I did. Aunt Nancy and Uncle Danny had been there, too, but now they had gone to greet some of the mourners and talk to the funeral director about something. Max Levene is dead, I thought, so what could possibly matter?

My mother was at the front of the room. She'd been standing by the coffin silently, rigidly. Like a soldier standing guard. Markie was kind of crouched behind my father, as if he could hide from what was happening.

Suddenly Ma's body convulsed as if a bolt of lightning had struck her. She started sobbing. Dad rushed up to her and held her. He touched her cheeks with a handkerchief.

"Oy, my God," Nana screamed.

Markie spun around and stared at Nana. His eyes were full of fright. Poor Mark, I thought. I wanted to go and put an arm around him and tell him that everything would be okay.

But my orders were plain.

"David, stay with your grandmother," Dad had said on the drive over. "Take care of Nana, that's your job. You're a young man now and I'm counting on you."

A young man. I'm thirteen, and with Max dead I felt as if I were five again.

Nana moaned louder than before. It was a chilling sound. "Don't cry, Nana," I pleaded. "Please don't cry."

She moaned again. I jumped to my feet.

"I can't take this," I yelled.

"David!" my father said, "get a grip on yourself."

"I'm sorry," I said, and I dashed out of the room, feeling as if something were chasing me.

I ran through the lobby. It was filled with people who had loved Max Levene. But not like me, I thought; they didn't love Grampa the way I loved him. When I spotted the men's room, I hurried in, praying that it would be empty. I needed to be alone. The room was empty—and white and gleaming, and so clean you could probably perform surgery in it. Heart surgery, I thought sadly.

"Damn it, Max," I shouted. "Damn you. Why did you have to die? I didn't do anything wrong."

My words didn't make any sense, but they felt right. I pounded my fists in the air as if there were ghosts that I had to fight off.

After a minute I was exhausted. I bent over the sink and splashed cold water on my face. "Dummy," I told myself. "It's not as if no one told you Grampa was dying. Everyone knew. Even Grampa. Especially Grampa."

"You must not upset yourself, Duvid," I heard Max say again in my mind, as he had so many times. "Be happy, not sad. You hear what I'm telling you? Your heart must be filled with good things, not this business of dying."

That was easy for him to say. He wasn't the one being left behind.

I kept staring at myself in the mirror. But I kept

4

seeing Max. "He's a regular little Max Levene," everyone always said. "The image."

I felt as if a lump the size of a tennis ball had gotten caught in my throat, and when I tried to swallow, my eyes stung and a strange sound erupted in the room. It was a big booming cry, as if someone were in awful pain, and it echoed across the slick tile walls of the men's room. A moment passed before I realized the sound was me crying. It was being wrenched out of me like a tumor, and to me it was as frightening as Nana's wailing. When it was gone, I felt as if someone had been choking me and had finally stopped, and the tears rushed out of me like water from the faucet.

When I stopped crying, I splashed more water on my face. While I was drying myself I saw my reflection in the mirror. Markie was standing behind me.

"How long have you been there?" I asked.

"It's okay," Markie said. "You had to cry sooner or later. Dad sent me to get you. They're starting the service."

"Damn."

"You okay now?" Markie said.

"Yeah. You?"

"I guess," he said, but he sounded pathetic. As we stepped into the lobby I put an arm around Markie's shoulder.

In the chapel I found Nana sitting in the first row with the rest of the family. I sat beside her again, feeling now as if I understood the strange sounds she had made.

The chapel was packed. I turned around to see

Max's friends. Max sure was loved. A couple of rows back I saw my best friend, Randy. He smiled sadly. Even Randy came, I thought. I waved to him. My father leaned across Nana and snapped at me. "Turn around and pay attention," he whispered.

"I know."

"Shh."

I couldn't believe it. What did Dad think, that I didn't care? Nobody loves Max Levene more than I do.

Did.

I sat quietly while the rabbi talked about what a great guy Max was.

And then it hit me.

That face. I had seen that face.

I peeked over my shoulder and looked for it again. It had been there, right near Randy. Yes, there it was. That white fluffy hair, those white bushy eyebrows, the thin, bony nose. For an instant the man's eyes met mine. Then he shifted in his seat and he was out of view. My heart pounded. It was Bernie Bauer. "B.B."

I was sure of it.

CHAPTER TWO

I would probably never have heard of B.B. if we hadn't gone to Newburyport last summer. And I probably wouldn't have gone to Newburyport if I weren't so short. At least that's how it seemed at the time.

Let me explain.

See, I love basketball, and last summer, when I was twelve, there was an intermediate basketball league for kids eleven to thirteen in Worcester County, Massachusetts, which is where I live, and there was a team from my town, Westbridge. On the morning when they posted the names of the kids who had made the team, I bicycled over to the playground. I read the list over and over. The list was alphabetical, and David Newman, that's me, should have been tucked right in between Arty Neilson and Lenny Rich. It wasn't. Unbelievable. I don't know if it's possible for a blank space to be ugly, but that space between Neilson and Rich was the ugliest thing I ever saw. I had been left out. Ignored. I felt as if someone had smacked me in the stomach with a battering ram.

The kids playing on the court were watching me. It seemed as if everybody in the world, and probably even people from other planets, knew I had been left off the team. I swallowed hard. There was no way I was going to let those kids see me cry, so I jumped back on my bike.

All the way home I bit my lip. The worst of it was knowing the reason I had been left off the team. My height. I was too short. Everybody figured my shots would be blocked and that other kids would be able to shoot over me because I was such a shrimp. But they were wrong. I guess they never heard of Spud Webb. Or Isiah Thomas, for that matter. It wasn't fair. I hated being short.

"Great news, David," my mother said when I trudged into the house. "We're going to Newburyport."

Ma was lugging a basket of laundry up from the basement and smiling. She didn't seem to notice that I was having the worst day of my life.

"Where the heck is Newburyport?" I asked.

"Right here in Massachusetts. About an hour and a half drive. It's on the coast, near New Hampshire."

8

"Why would we want to go there?" I said.

Ma doesn't like to waste time, so she sat at the dining room table and folded laundry while she talked. "Because your Uncle Danny has already paid to rent a cottage for two weeks and now he and Nancy have to go to Colorado on business, so lucky us, we get it."

"Yeah," I said. "Lucky us."

"You can go swimming every day. We'll be right on Plum Island."

"Plum Island, dumb island," I said.

"Cute," Ma said. "Real cute."

Ma still couldn't see what a rotten mood I was in. She was really into this laundry folding thing. "Your father will only come up on weekends," she continued, "because he's got to go to the office, and Markie will stay at music camp. We've already spent a fortune on that, so he won't be able to go with us either. But Nana and Grampa will be with us. And we can all just relax and read books and not do any housework and . . ." Then she looked at me. "Oh, David, I'm sorry," she said, finally noticing my mood. "You didn't make the team, did you?"

"No," I said. "Too short."

I told Ma how lousy I felt, and she hugged me for a while.

"I know you feel awful, honey, but at least it means we'll have a good time at Plum Island."

"Huh?" I said. Sometimes Ma's way of thinking isn't exactly like other people's.

"Well, isn't it obvious?" she said. "If you had made

the basketball team, you wouldn't want to go to Plum Island. But for some reason it's important for you to go, so the chief elf arranged for you not to make the basketball team."

"Great," I said. "Be sure to thank him for me."

The "chief elf" is Ma's way of saying God sometimes. If something is really serious, like someone is sick or hurt, she'll say God, but if it's something like me not making the basketball team, or the time she didn't get the lead in *Auntie Mame*, she says the chief elf did it, and he had a good reason. Ma says there are elves all over the place, good elves who put quarters on the sidewalk for us to find, and pixie elves who make us spill glasses of milk or trip on our shoelaces. I always thought elves were Irish, not Jewish, but Ma says it's leprechauns that are Irish, and that it's a well-known fact that twenty-seven percent of all elves are Jewish. Dad and Markie and I have never been completely sure if Ma believes this stuff or not.

Max and Nana came over that night, and we packed everything, including my bicycle, into Ma's red Subaru wagon. In the morning we were ready to go. Nana and Ma drove off in the station wagon. Max and I followed in Max's "pride and joy"—that's what he called it—his 1957 Buick.

After I had strapped on my seat belt, Max said what he always said when I got into his car.

"Now this, Duvid, is a car. Built like a tank. Today they don't make cars like this. Runs like the day I bought it."

Then I said what I always said.

"When did you buy it, Max? Yesterday?"

It was good to be with Max again, even though I had to worry about him getting lost if Ma took any sudden turns. Max and I had always been great pals, but lately it seemed as if I hadn't seen as much of him as I had when I was little. Max lived in Newton, about forty miles away, and I was always busy with school and my friends, and basketball and bicycling. But Max still called me. Every week.

As we drove along Route 117 toward the interstate Max let me shift gears on the old Buick. Every time we came to a stop, Max put his foot on the clutch and shouted out, "Max Levene to copilot. Prepare for takeoff. First gear," and I grabbed the shiny plastic ball at the top of the gearshift, and pulled it into first gear. Then we built up some speed, and Max called out "second gear," then "third gear," and finally after we were really moving along, "fourth gear."

"What'cha talking, Max Levene?" I said. "There's no fourth gear on this car."

"Oh, yes, I forgot," he said, smiling ever so slightly.

As we drove up Interstate 495, following Ma's Subaru, Max told me about the projects he was working on around the house—Max loved to tinker—and the books he was reading and all the food Nana had packed. "Nana brings enough in case an army should drop by for lunch," he said.

"That's Nana," I said, and I told him about being too short for the basketball team, and the dumb movie Randy and I had seen, and all the things that seemed

11

important. Then we played word games, which we always did on long drives. We played the alphabet game. Max had to find something along the highway that began with the letter *A*, like "apple tree," then I had to find a *B*, and so on. Whenever we played this game and Max got stuck, he'd try to trick me. He'd make up a word and claim it was Yiddish, because he spoke Yiddish and I didn't, but I could tell it was just some nutty word he'd made up.

So we're driving along 495, and we got to *M*, and it was Max's turn. I could tell he was stuck. I could see his sneaky old eyes shifting back and forth while he tried to figure out how he was going to trick me.

"Anytime this month will be fine, Max," I said.

"Soon," he said. "Soon I will see something. Hmm. Let me see . . . oh, look, Duvid, quick over there; it's a *mahooblisheh!*"

I turned to see it, but Max said, "Oh, too late; we passed it."

"What'cha talking, Max Levene?" I said. "You didn't see any *mahooblisheh*; there's no such thing."

"Oh, yes, Duvid," Max said with a straight face. "It was out there by the side of the road. It was a big *mahooblisheh*, green it was, and it had, I think, an extra long handle yet."

I was trying not to laugh. "Yeah? Well, then, what exactly is a *mahooblisheh*?"

"Well, my grandson, this is difficult to explain. I don't know the English word for this thing. Maybe you should take your grandfather's word for it."

12

I couldn't stand it anymore. I started shrieking with laughter the way I used to when I was six years old and Max would tickle my belly. Max was hilarious, the way he pretended to take it so seriously, never cracking a smile.

"Okay, Grampa," I said when I stopped laughing. "I'm going to accept *mahooblisheh*. But the next time you see something weird along the road with a Yiddish name, we're going to back all the way up to it and take a real good look. Okay?"

"What you suggest is very dangerous," Max said. "This backing up. No, this we must not do." Then he looked at me and just barely smiled. "A boy should learn to trust his grampa," he said, patting my knee, which of course set me off on another round of giggles.

When we got to Newburyport, we followed Ma straight on through to the other side, where she drove over the causeway that leads to Plum Island.

"This island, Duvid, is approximately eleven miles long, but narrow, very narrow. Most of it is a bird sanctuary, which is good. The birds should have someplace to go where they won't be bothered, no? But there are many cottages, also, and restaurants. You'll see."

"Max, you sound like a *National Geographic* Special. How do you know so much about Plum Island?"

Max glanced at me. I noticed that he looked tired. When I was little, Max could drive forever. Now after an hour and a half he seemed real weary. "You'd be surprised what a person can learn by picking up a book," he said. "You have picked up some good books lately?"

"A few," I said. I was ashamed to tell him that I had read only one book all year, *Giant Steps*, by Kareem Abdul-Jabbar. "Biographies mostly," I added.

Ma's Subaru took a left and we followed. I couldn't see the ocean, but I could smell it, and between cottages I could see long stretches of sand that went up and then down. I knew there were beaches just beyond the hills. Ma took another left, down a narrow and bumpy unpaved road.

"Ah, a real beach community," Max said. "We'll have a good time."

Now I was getting excited. Maybe Ma was right—maybe something good would happen while we were on Plum Island. The road got even narrower and sandier. On both sides there were cute little cottages, all different colors and sitting at different angles, as if they had just been dropped from the sky. I glanced into the small yards beside the cottages, hoping to see a basketball rim. Maybe I'd find some kids to play basketball with. I counted cottages. After we passed twelve of them, Ma pulled up in front of a green wooden cottage that had a big white door, and white trim around the windows. Max pulled the old Buick in beside her. The cottage was a riot. It was big and kind of lopsided, with a black shingle roof that was much steeper on one side than on the other. The door was slightly tilted. None of the windows was exactly the same as another, and the front porch sagged like a hammock.

"Very nice," Max said, "very nice."

"Yeah," I said, "it looks like something out of a cartoon."

After Ma and I unloaded the cars, Max stood in the big downstairs living room in front of the two sliding glass doors that looked out on the inlet behind the house. Beyond him I could see a catamaran with a big red sail bobbing in the water, and there were also some people in a rowboat.

"Duvid, you look exhausted," Max said. "I'd better take a nap." I giggled. "You explore the beach, and I will explore that sofa over there." "Sofa" is what Max always called a couch.

Almost as soon as I left the house, I felt sad again. Maybe that's because I didn't have Max Levene to take my mind off the basketball team. On the way to the beach, which was only a two-minute walk, I looked around for some other kids. But nobody was outside. It was cool and the sky had gone gray, and now and then a drop of icy rain stung my face. I knew I couldn't go swimming, but I wanted to see the beach.

The beach was practically empty. For as far as I could see in either direction, sand and ocean stretched to the horizon. The only people around were a guy and girl holding hands and a couple of kids flying a kite. The few people I could see in the distance were like black specks against the silvery gray sky. Huge waves banged against the shore, and I could tell a storm was coming. About a half mile away there was a jetty, a long line of huge boulders that looked like a giant black finger pointing out into the ocean. I decided to walk to it. I pulled off my Nikes and socks and walked to the edge of the water. I usually like the feel of my feet slapping against the smooth, shiny mud where the water meets the sand, but when I stuck my foot in the water, it was freezing, and I let out such a shriek, you would have sworn I'd been attacked by a killer shark or something.

I kept my eye on the jetty as I walked toward it. I still felt lousy, and the crummy weather wasn't exactly cheering me up. Even the water, with no sun on it, looked black and inky. I thought about the basketball team and how much fun the other kids would have without me. While I was walking I passed a couple of teenage boys who weren't wearing any shirts even though it was cold, probably so they could show off their great physiques. I don't blame them. If I had big muscles, I probably wouldn't wear a shirt either. When they walked by me, I heard one of them say, "Yeah, well I'm going to be fourteen next month, so I don't need anybody telling me what to do." Not even fourteen yet, and they were both about a foot taller than me. I felt worse than before.

When I got to the jetty, I climbed onto a big flat rock and sat there with my legs dangling over the edge, and closed my eyes. Sometimes when I'm alone, I make up basketball games in my mind. Usually it's a championship game, and I always score a lot of points, and I get rebounds even though I'm no taller in make-believe than I am in real life. I was going in for a dazzling behind-the-back lay-up against the two kids with the muscles, when I felt something slimy . . . like a jellyfish . . . rubbing against my foot. "Yipes!" I shouted. My eyes flew open. I yanked my feet up.

It was a dog, a little black Labrador with big floppy ears. In her mouth she had a chunk of driftwood with strands of seaweed hanging from it. That's what had been rubbing against my leg. The dog dropped the wood, stared up at me with big brown eyes, and whined, as if to say hello. She looked as lonely as I felt.

"Hi, pup; you want someone to play with, don't you?" I said. I jumped down from the rock, and she rubbed her head against my leg. I felt as if I'd made a friend. She wagged her tail and pushed the driftwood against my feet with her nose. I picked it up and hurled it as far as I could. "Go get it, girl." The dog loped off happily, tossing up sand under her paws, and then she turned around and brought the piece of wood back to me. I threw it again. She fetched it again. I decided to call her Rachel. A pretty name for a pretty dog.

After I had thrown the stick ten times, Rachel was tired. I sat on the rock again, and Rachel climbed up and lay down beside me.

It was peaceful there, with Rachel pressed against me and the sea gulls squawking in the sky. If it had been warm and sunny, I could have sat there for hours. But it was getting cooler, and I could see that it would soon be raining. I was restless. When Rachel was asleep, I decided to walk all the way to the end of the jetty.

I rubbed Rachel's neck one last time, and then I started walking. The rocks on the top of the jetty were flat and wide, so I knew it was safe. I made my way easily. The waves splashed against the rocks below me and sprayed my legs with cold water.

When I was about halfway along the jetty, I turned to see Rachel. She was awake, staring at me, wagging her tail.

"Stay there, girl," I called. "I'll be back."

I stopped about six feet from the end of the jetty and stared out at the sea as if I were Balboa or Cortés or one of those guys discovering a new ocean. The water sprayed me, and the wind blew at my hair. I felt tall.

Something brushed against my feet. I looked down. It was Rachel. She nuzzled my leg, then went dashing toward the end of the jetty where the rocks began to slope down. She tried to turn and run back toward me, but her paws kept sliding out from under her on the slippery rocks.

"No, girl, you shouldn't be out here," I said. I moved cautiously toward the end of the jetty and reached down for her, but she slipped before I could grab her. She fell backward. I watched her hit the water, and the splash that followed was the most sickening sound I have ever heard.

"Rachel," I screamed, and she let out a yelp. She started paddling wildly, but the waves kept pushing her against the rocks. For a second the rocks were stained with blood where her face had hit them, and then the next wave washed the ugly redness away. The wave after that pulled her away. My heart raced. I tried to climb down to get her but the rocks were slippery and I kept losing my footing. I was sure that if I managed to get down there I'd bash my head and get killed. I was desperate. I wanted to dive in and save Rachel, but the rocks stretched out a long way beneath me. I felt helpless.

"Rachel," I screamed. She was being pulled farther and farther away.

"Rachel, Rachel," I cried. I faced the shore. "Help!" I called, but there were only a few people on the beach, and they were so far away, they couldn't see me or hear me. Besides, there was nothing they could do. I was the only person close to Rachel. I was the one who should do something. But I didn't know what to do. The wind was blowing like crazy. Rachel was becoming smaller and smaller in the distance, and then I couldn't even see her at all.

For a long time I stood there, just in a daze.

"It didn't happen," I said out loud. "It didn't happen. It could not have happened; it didn't happen, David; it didn't happen," as if by saying it enough times I could make it true. "It didn't happen; it just didn't happen," I said over and over as I made my way back along the jetty to the beach.

CHAPTER THREE

As I trudged back toward the place where I had left my sneakers I looked out over the acres of water. My body ached, and my heart was still pounding something awful. Hoping to spot Rachel, I stared so hard that my eyes burned. I searched the beach, too, thinking that somehow Rachel had gotten back to shore. Yes, I thought, she was probably pushed in by the tide just like a bottle with a note in it, and any second I would see her running toward me, probably with a stick in her mouth. But as far as I could see in either direction, nothing moved on the beach. I was alone.

"Rachel!" I called, "Rachel!"

By the time I got my sneakers on and crossed the

street, I was thinking that Rachel would be at the cottage waiting for me. I knew that didn't make any sense. She wasn't my puppy and she didn't know where I lived, but when I crossed onto our street, I started to run anyhow, half expecting to see her.

When I got to the cottage, Ma was setting the table for supper and Nana was leaning over the stove, pouring salt into her hand, which she sprinkled into a pot of soup one grain at a time, as if it were gold. Max was still on the couch in the living room, but now he was reading.

"Ma, you didn't see a dog around, did you?" I asked. "A black Lab."

"No, why?"

"Nothing," I said. "Just wondering."

All through supper I didn't say a word. You would have thought I was a monk who'd taken a vow of silence or something. Ma asked me what was wrong.

"Shortness," I grunted, and that seemed to satisfy her. She figured I was still upset about not making the team.

After supper I sat on the deck facing the inlet behind the house. The storm clouds had blown right over us without dumping any rain, and now the sun was shining on the water. Near the shore a woman with a baby on her lap splashed in an inner tube, and farther out there were two catamarans with teenagers hanging on them, laughing and trying to knock one another over. It seemed as if everybody in the world was happy, except me. Why did bad things always happen to me, I wondered. Yesterday I had been left off the team; today I had accidentally killed a puppy. It didn't seem fair that I was always the one who had bad luck. I was mad at the chief elf. Was this the thing I had come to Plum Island for, to watch a puppy drown?

I heard the glass door slide open behind me, and Max Levene came out on the deck. He had taken a shower and was wearing a new short-sleeve plaid shirt and another pair of those baggy khaki pants that he loved and that I thought were a riot. When he sat down in the lawn chair next to mine, the smell of his after-shave filled the air between us, and I remembered suddenly what it felt like to be four years old and sitting on Max's lap.

"So?" he said. "You are still sad?"

"Sad? What'cha talking, Max, I'm not sad," I said. But my voice sounded phony, the way it does when you try to act in a school play and you're not very good.

"What happened when you went for a walk that makes you so sad?"

"Nothing," I said. "I was just thinking about being left off the basketball team."

"Hmmn," Max said.

When Max said "Hmmn," it meant "keep going, you haven't told me everything."

"Don't give me 'hmmn,' " I said.

He reached over and took my hand. For the first time ever his hand felt old and weak to me, as if I could actually hurt it if I tried. "Sometimes you can fool your mother," he said, "but Max Levene you don't fool so good. What happened?"

If he hadn't touched me, I probably wouldn't have cried, but he squeezed my hand, and the tears rolled down my cheek. I told him about Rachel.

"She died, Grampa, and it's my fault."

"No, Duvid, it's not your fault," Max said. "But you have a good reason to be sad. It's good to talk about these things, not keep them inside you."

For a long time we were quiet. Max gave me a handkerchief to dry my tears. Then he said, "Come, we'll go to town now."

"Town. What for?"

"What do you think?" Max said. "Ice cream. What else?"

We got in Max's old Buick and drove across the causeway to Newburyport, with me as copilot, shifting gears. It only took five minutes to get there. Newburyport was much noisier than Plum Island. It was seven o'clock and Newburyport was as busy as in the middle of the day. People, tourists mostly, were buzzing in and out of clothing stores, restaurants, bookshops, antique stores, and all kinds of specialty shops. I had saved up enough money for a new baseball bat, so I looked around for a sports store, but I didn't see one. Most of the shops looked freshly painted, and almost all of them had bright colors and small windows, and hand-painted signs hanging over the door.

Of course there was lots of traffic. As usual, Max got confused by the traffic and started honking his horn and calling "let me through, let me through." When he saw a parking lot, he waved his hand frantically out the window and took a sudden left turn from the right lane.

"Close call," he muttered as we pulled in behind a row of red brick buildings. "Almost missed it."

We walked over to State Street and found an ice cream shop called Annabelle's. They had dozens of flavors, all written on a big blackboard. Max studied it carefully.

"Cookies and cream," he said. "Now that sounds very good." Then, "Chocolate royal. Sounds tasty, doesn't it, Duvid?" And so on, all down the list even though we both knew that Max was going to get vanilla, the way he always did. Finally he pressed his hands together as if he had just closed some big business deal. "Duvid," he said, "I have made a decision. This time I will get vanilla."

"Really, Max?" I said. "I'm amazed that you would choose vanilla."

"Yes, well, I do this to surprise you," he said. "And you, what do you get, one of these *meshuggeneh* new flavors that take longer to say than they do to eat?"

Meshuggeneh is a Yiddish word for crazy. "Coconut," I said. "Large. In a sugar cone."

As we walked along State Street, licking our ice-cream cones, I noticed that all the downtown buildings were made out of brick, red brick mostly.

"Grampa, there're no wooden buildings here," I said. "That's weird."

"Not so weird," he said. "They had a fire here. It

was many years ago. The town burned to the ground, you see, and so the people decided it would be a smart thing to build again from bricks so in case of fire, the houses wouldn't burn.''

"How do you know all this?''

"Last night I read it in a book. It is good to know the history of a place.''

We stopped at the end of the street and stared into the window of an art gallery.

"When we get home, I will show you the book,'' Max said. "It has lots of pictures.'' He wiped some ice cream from his face with a napkin and looked around. Then he glanced again into the art gallery window, and his body went stiff, and he had to grab my arm to keep from falling.

"Oh, my, Duvid,'' he said, "this cannot be.''

"Grampa, what is it? What's wrong?''

"Quick, take this,'' Grampa said. He shoved his ice-cream cone into my hand and rushed into the art gallery.

Through the window I watched him talk excitedly to a skinny gray-haired lady behind the counter. Max kept thrusting his hands through the air like an orchestra conductor, asking questions and jabbing his finger toward a large painting in the window. Finally the woman came over. She pulled the painting out of the window and showed it to Max. He stared at it for a long time, real close, the way he did when he was sewing—Max was a tailor, and even though he was retired, he still did a lot of sewing. Then he asked the woman some more questions. She shook her head

25

and put the painting back in the window. I studied the painting to see what the commotion was all about.

It was a picture of a copper pot, some wooden candlesticks, a bunch of grapes, and a lobster—what Ma calls a still life, except when she does one, it's of even weirder things, like one time she painted a picture of all the shoes in her closet. The lobster painting was pretty good, I guess, though personally I'd rather have a picture of Kevin McHale going in for a lay-up.

I looked in the lower right-hand corner of the painting—that's where Ma always signs hers—to see who had painted it. There was no name, only a picture of a bee with fluttering wings that looked real.

When Max stepped out on the sidewalk, he was all excited, as if he were going to have a heart attack or something.

"Here, calm down; eat some ice cream," I said. I handed him his vanilla cone, which was starting to drip all over me. "What the heck is going on?"

"I don't know," Max said.

"You don't know?"

"Well, I am not positive," he said, "but it seems to me that that painting was by someone I knew very well."

"Really? Who?"

"Bernie."

"You had a friend named Bernie?"

"Yes." Max glanced at the painting one last time, then put an arm around me. "Duvid, over there. We sit. We talk." He led me across the street to Market Square, where there was a wide area of red bricks and lots of benches. This was sort of the center of New-buryport, where you could sit and eat ice cream and watch people go by.

The only empty bench had half a dozen pigeons on it. Max said, "Excuse me, pigeons, but my grand-son and I must talk." He waved a hand at them, and they flapped their wings and flew off toward the other side of the square. "Thank you very much. Have a good flight," he called.

"Okay," I said, "so you think your friend Bernie painted the picture in the window. But how come? There's no name on it. I looked."

"Did you see the bee?" Max asked.

"Yeah." I laughed. "Is that his name, Bernie Bee?"

Max didn't laugh. "No. Bernie Bauer. We called him B.B. So he always used two bees for his signature."

"But, Grampa, there was only one bee."

"So, what difference, it's the same idea."

"Well, it's not exactly the same, Grampa. I mean one bee is not the same as two."

"Listen to me, Duvid," Max snapped. He seemed upset. "It is not just the bee. It is the style, the way of painting. It is the same. This you understand?"

"I understand," I said. "You don't have to yell at me."

"Forgive me. It is . . . this man was my friend."

"Well, what did the lady say?"

Max swiped at the air in front of him as if he were trying to scoot away some more pigeons. "Ahh, she's a *schlemiel*; she knows nothing. She is—what is this

27

you say?—yes, a bimbo!" He laughed. "In the old days the clerks in the store, they knew what they were selling. Today they are robots, that is all. I say to her, 'Who paints this painting?'—she says, 'I don't know.' I say to her, 'How long has this painting been here?'— she says 'I don't know.' I say to her, 'How much does this painting cost?' This, she knows."

"How much was it, Grampa?"

"Five hundred dollars."

"Whew! That's a lot of bananas."

"Bananas? What do you mean, bananas?"

"It's just an expression, Max Levene."

Max shook his head. "The owner is due back at the end of this week. Then I will find out for certain."

We finished our ice-cream cones and walked back to the parking lot. Max beeped his way into traffic, and we headed for Plum Island. Max didn't seem very happy, and he didn't ask me to be copilot.

"Max," I said, after he had been quiet for a long time, "who is B.B.?"

"He was my best friend when I was a boy in Germany."

"But you lived in Poland when you were a kid."

"When I was seven, my father moved us to Germany, to Heidelberg, because he knew a man who wanted to be his partner. They supplied shoemakers. That is when I met Bernie. We were always together after that. Best friends."

"Like me and Randy," I said.

"Yes, like you and Randy. We did not play basketball, but we were very good with the ice skates."

28

I laughed. "Come on, Grampa. You on ice skates?"

Max smiled for the first time. "I was not always an old man, you know." Then he looked ahead and smiled as if he were watching a film of something he remembered. "Oh, yes, Bernie and Max, we were the best. We could skate fast, we could spin, we could skate backward, yet."

"What else did you do?" It was fascinating to think of Max being a kid like me once.

"We did everything," Max said. "We climbed, we ran, we chased the girls. Ah, but when my little sister died, Mama was never the same, and my father moved the family back to Vilna, in Poland. We packed up everything we had, but Bernie and I, we made a vow that when we were older, we would go into business together, somehow."

"And did you?"

"Yes." Max smiled. "Bernie came with his wife to Vilna. Jacqueline. Such a beautiful girl you never saw. She was English. It was she who gave Bernie the name 'B.B.' They had an apartment, and we pooled our money, and we started a tailor shop."

"Bernie was a tailor, too?"

"Ah, Duvid, he was a terrible tailor. You should never bring your clothes to such a tailor. But Bernie could paint. He was a regular Rembrandt."

"So, what ever happened to him?"

Max didn't answer. His eyes seemed to go dark, as if someone had gotten inside his head and turned off a lamp.

"Grampa?"

He twitched his shoulders. "So," he said. "Enough about your grandfather. Tell me about you. You have a girlfriend yet?"

"No, Max, I don't have a girlfriend yet; now tell me about B.B."

"It was a long time ago, Duvid, a long time ago. It was a different time, a different world then." He turned just long enough to stare at me, with this terrible sadness in his eyes.

"We will talk no more about B.B. Not tonight," he said, and when he said it, he sounded so cold that he scared me.

CHAPTER FOUR

When I went to bed that night, I thought about Sparky, my cat who disappeared when I was eight years old. I remembered how I had spent a week going up and down every street in Westbridge calling "Sparky, Sparky," and how awful I felt at the end of each day.

I didn't want somebody to have to do that for Rachel, always getting his hopes up and then getting disappointed. So on Monday morning I decided I had to find Rachel's owner and tell him what had happened.

"Where are you going?" Nana called as I tried to sneak out the cottage door at eight o'clock. As usual, she sounded as if she were accusing me of a major felony.

"Out," I said.

"Come sit. I'll make you some breakfast," Nana said. She stood there, all five feet of her, waving a spatula in the air as if she would use it to clobber the next twelve-year-old boy who tried to leave the house.

"But I'm not hungry."

"What do you mean you're not hungry?"

"I mean I'm like, you know, not hungry."

"Of course you're hungry," Nana said. She aimed the spatula at a kitchen chair. "Sit," she said.

I sat. Then Nana started fixing breakfast, all the time mumbling to herself things like "the boy eats like a bird. No wonder he doesn't grow."

"Where's Max?" I said.

"Max, Max?" she said. "I don't know this man."

"Okay, *Grampa*," I said. Nana's the only one in the family who didn't like me to call Grampa "Max."

"Your grandfather is out for a walk with your mother."

"Did you make him eat?"

"I don't have to make your grandfather eat. Your grandfather loves my cooking."

"Nana, everybody loves your cooking," I said. "It's just that there's so much of it."

Nana made me enough French toast to feed half the people in Paris. As usual, the smell of food cooking made me decide that I was hungry, after all. But I was anxious to find Rachel's owner and get it over

32

with. After I ate the French toast and gulped down a glass of milk, I dashed for the door.

"Thanks, Nana. I'd love to help you with the dishes, but I got to run," I said.

"So where are you rushing off to, already?"

"No place," I said, closing the screen door behind me.

I still hadn't told Ma or Nana about Rachel. I didn't know why exactly. It just seemed embarrassing.

"David, wait," Nana called. She came to the door, opened it a crack, and slipped two crumpled-up dollar bills into my hand, the way she often does. "You might need some spending money," she said with a smile. "Don't tell your grandfather."

"Thanks, Nana," I said.

I jumped off the porch and scrambled onto the sandy road, walking so fast that I was almost running. Think logically, I told myself. If I had lost a dog, where would I go to look for it? When I got to the corner across from the beach I turned left and walked to The Nautilus, which is a shop that sells submarine sandwiches and soda, and sunglasses, suntan lotion, radio batteries, and all the other stuff you need for the beach.

The woman behind the counter at The Nautilus was named Kay. I could tell because she had a big nametag pinned to her waitress uniform. She was big and heavy, with lots of blond hair flowing in all directions. Her cheeks were as red as berries.

"What can I do for you, handsome?" she said.

"Who me?" I said.

"You're the only gorgeous-looking young man I see in here," she said, with a wink, "and believe me, I've been looking."

Actually, I was the only person in there. Not too many people eat submarine sandwiches at eight thirty in the morning.

"Well, I was wondering if you know anybody who lost a dog."

Her eyes widened. "Pinky!" she said.

"Uh. No," I said. "This dog is a black Labrador."

"Yes. That's Pinky," she said. "You found her? You found Pinky?"

"Sort of," I said. I started to tell her. "She was playing on the beach and—"

"Oh, that's great! Candy will be so happy. Where did you find her?"

"On the beach," I said. I couldn't seem to tell her the truth.

"Well, that's wonderful," Kay said. "Candy's been looking all over for that dog."

"Candy?"

"She owns Pinky."

"Where does she live?"

"Over on Taylor Street. About halfway down the road. It's a little brown cottage. A shack really. You'll see a couple of junked cars in the yard. But you won't find Candy there. She's still out looking for her dog. She was in here about twenty minutes ago. I think she went down toward the lighthouse."

"What does she look like?"

"About your age. Long black hair." Kay winked at me.

"Thanks," I said, and I rushed out before Kay could ask me any more questions about Rachel. Pinky.

A girl, I thought, as I headed toward the lighthouse. Why did it have to be a girl? She'd probably cry when I told her, and then what would I do? I never know what to do when people cry. I was wishing Max were with me. He'd know how to handle it.

I walked toward the lighthouse, which was at the end of Plum Island that juts into the Merrimack River. The street led right to a giant parking lot, and as I got close to it I heard one of my favorite sounds, the bouncing of a basketball. Basketball! There was a court! Suddenly my life seemed brighter. When I got into the parking lot, I could see the court off to the left. There were six kids playing on it. They were just shooting around, and two of them were talking to a girl who was asking questions. She was short. About twelve years old. Long black hair. It had to be Candy. The boys shook their heads, and she started walking away from them, toward where I was. I should have gone to her then, just walked right up to her and said, "Your dog is dead." Instead I turned and walked back the other way, pretending that I hadn't seen her.

After I went about twenty feet, my legs started to slow down, as if somebody were tugging at me. It was my conscience. You've got to tell her, David. I turned around, and there she was coming toward me. She was wearing jeans and an oversized pink

T-shirt that had a huge rainbow on it. She was moving real slowly because she was searching everyplace, even ridiculous places like parked cars.

When she got to me, she said "Hi." I was surprised to see her smile.

"Hi," I said.

"Have you seen a black dog?"

"Huh?" I was stalling.

"A black dog," she said. "My dog is lost."

I knew I had to do it now. I had to tell Candy that her dog was dead. My heart was pounding. "No," I said. I couldn't believe I had said that. "But if you want, I'll help you look for her. Or him, I mean. Whatever."

I felt like a liar. David, you *are* a liar, my conscience reminded me.

"That would be great," she said. "I've been looking all over. Her name is Pinky."

She told me her name was Candy, and I told her my name was David. We walked along for a while, looking everyplace, inside trash barrels, under bushes. When we came to a low brick building that used to be a bakery, Candy said, "Give me ten fingers," and she showed me how to link my hands together so she could step into them and hoist herself onto the roof and look around from there.

"Where are you from?" I asked after I had helped her down from the roof and we had started walking again.

"I live here," she said. "Plum Island."

"Oh. I didn't know anybody lived here. I thought everybody was just visiting."

"My mother runs a bait shop," she said. "You know, for catching fish."

"What about your father?"

"Dead," she said.

"Sorry."

"Oh, that's okay," she said. "He was a war hero. He got the Congressional Medal of Honor and everything."

"Really?"

"Well, of course really," she said. "You don't think I'd make up a story like that, do you?"

"No, no," I said. "I didn't mean anything."

"What about you?" she said. "Where are you from?"

"Westbridge," I said, which she had never heard of. Nobody has. I told her how my family happened to come to Plum Island, and I told her about getting left off the basketball team, and before long we were walking so close that I could smell the perfume or whatever it was she was wearing. We were being real friendly, but all the time I was uncomfortable because I felt as if I had practically murdered her dog personally and then lied about even seeing her.

"Did you have your dog long?" I asked.

"Since she was six weeks old. My mother bought her."

"Do you know how much she cost?" It was a stupid question, but I was nervous. Besides, I was thinking

37

that next year when I had my bar mitzvah I'd have lots of money and maybe then I could buy Candy a new dog.

"Whatever it was, it was a lot for my mother because she doesn't make much money."

"How come you named your dog Pinky?" I said.

"Pink's my favorite color."

"But your dog was black," I said.

"So?" She laughed. "What was I going to do, paint my dog?"

Then we both chuckled, but every minute that went by made me feel more and more like a skunk. I had to tell her the truth, but I didn't want to do it out on the sidewalk, with people driving by and everything.

"Do you want to go look for Pinky on the beach?" I said.

"She's not there. I looked."

"Yeah, but maybe she's there now," I said nervously. "Maybe she's looking for you."

"She's not there," Candy said.

"Let's go anyhow," I said. "I've got this feeling."

"Really?" Candy said. Her eyes brightened. "My mom gets feelings like that. Like one time she got this feeling that my aunt was in trouble, and my aunt called up that same day and she was in a car crash. She's all right now, though."

We walked to the beach, and when we were so far away that we couldn't even see anybody, I said, "Let's sit in the sand. I've got to talk to you about something."

"What?"

"It's about your dog," I said. Candy looked into my eyes, and it was like she knew I was going to say something horrible. She sat down in the sand, almost as if somebody had pushed her.

I sat beside her. "I lied," I said. "When I told you I didn't see your dog. I did see her. She was up on those rocks over there, and she fell into the water. She died."

Candy didn't say anything. She stared out at the ocean, and the tears began to slide down her face. "Are you sure?" she said.

Actually, I was only about ninety percent sure, but I knew if I said that, then Candy would spend the next year walking through people's yards calling "Pinky, Pinky."

"Yes," I said, figuring if Pinky was alive, she'd come home anyhow.

Then Candy did something that surprised me. She pulled close to me, slipped her arms around my waist and put her head on my shoulder, and cried.

"Thank you for telling me," she said. "You didn't have to. I know that must have been hard to do."

I felt like such a heel. I hadn't told her the true story about how it was partly my fault. But I couldn't do that. I just couldn't. Besides, I told myself, what difference did it make? The dog was dead, no matter how I told the story.

At first I was scared to put my arms around Candy. I didn't know if I was supposed to squeeze her tight or just sort of pat her or what. Nobody ever tells you about these things. Finally I put my arms around her. I could feel my shoulder getting wet from her tears, and I held her for a long time, just kind of patting her on the back and telling her I was sorry about her dog dying, and before long I was crying, too.

CHAPTER FIVE

"So anyhow, she put her head right here on my shoulder, and she cried for a long time," I said to Max. I was telling him about Candy. I didn't bother to tell him that I had cried, too. Max and I were in Annabelle's ice cream shop in Newburyport again. It seemed like we were always in Annabelle's. We had started calling it "Ice Cream Central," because every time we drove the Buick into town, which was a lot during those first few days, we'd end up in Annabelle's.

We'd drive over to Newburyport just for something we could do together. Max didn't want to go to the beach with me, and I wasn't real anxious to sit out on the deck reading books with him. So going to Newburyport was our "David and Max time." That's what we called it.

I think for Max the ice cream was just an excuse to look at the lobster painting again, because every time we'd get ice cream he would say "Come, now we must walk," and we would always end up in front of the art gallery, where Max would stare at the picture in the window and shake his head and say "This is the work of B.B. You will see, you will see." Max was real impatient because the owner wasn't going to be back until the weekend.

This time at Annabelle's I had gotten a hot fudge sundae with peppermint stick ice cream, marshmallow, whipped cream, pecans, a cherry, and jimmies. I couldn't just walk down the street eating a monstrosity like that, so Max and I sat at one of the little round, glass-topped tables next to the window, where we could look out at the people walking by on State Street. Max got his regular, a vanilla cone.

"So afterward I went back to Candy's house, and she showed me her collection of pulleys," I told him.

"Pulleys?"

"Yeah, you know, they're like metal things that you put a rope through so you can lift heavy things."

"Yes, yes, I know. This girl, she collects them?"

"Yeah. You'd be surprised how many different types there are. She's got big ones, little ones, brass ones . . ."

Max was staring at me. "Hmmn," he said.

42

"Grampa, you got to understand, Candy's a little different," I said. "She's not like other girls."

"I see."

"Anyhow, their house is neat. I mean, it's old, and they don't have a stereo or anything, but there's all kinds of interesting stuff because Candy's mother makes things, and Candy collects a lot of things."

"Like pulleys?"

"Right," I said. "And doorknobs, too. We played with those for a while."

"She sounds like a nice girl, this Kendy."

"Not Kendy. Candy. You know, like a Hershey bar."

"Yes, yes, this is what I said — Kendy," Max said. He peered at me over his ice-cream cone. I couldn't tell if he was joking with me or not. "So," he said, looking at me slyly, "you like this girl?"

"Yeah, I like her a lot," I said.

"I thought so."

"No, Max, not like that. I mean, I like her. You know, like a friend."

While I finished off my sundae Grampa just licked away at his vanilla ice-cream cone as if it were the last one he would ever have, and he stared off into space. He'd been doing a lot of that lately. While I scraped the end of my sundae from the edges of the bowl, I watched the people on State Street. It was about four in the afternoon, and there were lots of people. One old guy stopped to read the list of flavors printed on the window. He was a jolly-looking guy with a nice face that was red from the sun, and he had a rolled-up newspaper, which he kept tapping in his hand like a baton. He had silvery white hair and the bushiest white eyebrows I had ever seen. He noticed me looking at him, and he smiled. I smiled back. That's when Grampa turned around.

"My God," I heard Grampa say.

"Huh?"

Grampa's ice-cream cone fell from his fingers and splattered on the table. He didn't even notice.

"My God," he said again.

"Grampa, what's wrong?" It was scary.

Grampa didn't answer. He reached over and tapped the window. The man looked at him, and then at me, as if to ask "What does he want?" Max stared at him some more, and then suddenly bounded out of his chair as if someone had thrown a rope around him and yanked him out of it. He bolted toward the door. The man with the eyebrows jumped back from the window and put up his hands as if Grampa had gone mad and was going to attack him. Max got outside and lunged for the man. The man stepped back. Max reached out and grabbed his shoulder. The man pushed Max's hand away and jumped back even farther. He looked at Max, then at me. He had a frightened look on his face. Max leapt toward him. Then the man turned and started running down State Street. Max ran after him. "Stop, stop," he shouted. They were both running as fast as guys that age could go. It wasn't like Bird and Ainge on a fast break, but they were moving at a pretty good clip for old guys.

44

I ran outside and started chasing Max.

"Grampa, what's going on?" I shouted. Everybody was looking at us. Max didn't answer. He just kept chasing the guy.

About halfway down State Street the bushy-eyebrowed guy turned around to see if Max was still chasing him. He dropped his newspaper and bent to pick it up but then saw Max coming at him, and he dashed around the corner of one of those red brick buildings. When Max got to the corner, he stopped and clutched at his heart. He shoved an arm out against the wall to hold himself up because he was all worn out. He took deep breaths. I had almost caught up with Max when he took one last deep breath, then darted around the corner to start chasing some more.

"Max, don't," I cried. "You're going to hurt yourself!"

I kept running. About all I could hear was the sound of my sneakers slapping against the sidewalk. When I got to the corner, I picked up the man's newspaper and shoved it into my back pocket, thinking he might want it if we ever caught up with him.

As soon as I turned the corner, which led onto a narrow brick lane between two buildings, I crashed into a woman who had two shopping bags of clothes. The clothes flew off in all directions. "Sorry, miss, sorry," I said. I wanted to stop and help pick up her stuff, but I was worried about Max, so I kept running. At the other end of the alley was a courtyard, with a small playground and several benches. Max was sitting on a bench with his head down. He was clutching his chest and gasping to catch his breath.

"Grampa, Grampa, are you all right?" I said. I could hear that my voice was high-pitched, the way it gets when I'm scared.

Max could hardly talk. He grabbed my arm and pointed across the courtyard to another alley that led to another street.

"Run, Duvid, run. You must find him."

"Grampa, I practically knocked some woman down back there. I better go back and help her pick up her stuff."

"Later, Duvid. Go. Find him."

"But what about you?"

"I'll be okay. Go. Catch him."

I didn't know what I was supposed to do with the guy once I caught him, but there wasn't any sense in asking Max. So I took off down the alley as fast I could run. When I got to the other side, I looked both ways. I'd come to the busy street in Newburyport again, with a lot of traffic, but there was no sign of the bushy-eyebrowed guy. I was too late. He had gotten away.

I trudged back to where Max was sitting.

"I lost him," I said. I sat on the bench beside Max.

"*Vay iz mir!*" Max said. He put an arm around me. He was starting to look more normal.

"It was him, Duvid, I know it was him."

"Who, Max?"

"My friend Bernie Bauer."

"B.B? The man who painted the lobster?"

"Yes, B.B. It cannot be, yet it is."

"It probably wasn't him," I said. "It was probably some guy who just looked like him."

"It was him," Max said.

"When was the last time you saw B.B.?"

"Forty years ago."

"Grampa, that's a long time. How can you be sure, if it's a guy you haven't seen in forty years?"

"Because you don't forget a face," Max said. "Not the face of your best friend, that you don't forget. It's in the eyes, Duvid, in the eyes."

"So why did he run?" I said.

"I don't know." Max sounded sad. "I don't know."

"Grampa, it's getting chilly. We'd better go."

I held Max's hand as we walked back through the alley and across State Street to our regular parking place. I looked for the lady with the shopping bags, but fortunately she was gone. I would have been embarrassed to face her.

After Max and I had been driving for a few minutes, I felt as if I were sitting on something. Then I realized it was the rolled-up newspaper.

"The guy dropped this," I said to Max.

"What is it?" Max said. He stared straight out at the traffic. I couldn't tell if he was watching for other cars or just thinking about the past.

"A newspaper," I said as I unrolled it. Then I looked at it closely. "Only it's not like a regular newspaper. It says Racing Form, whatever that is."

"Racing Form?" Max shouted. He yanked the steering wheel, swerving way over to the right, barely missing the cars that were parked there. He stomped his foot on the brake, and we came to a halt, with the rear end of the car still jutting out into traffic. Right away horns started blaring.

"Let me see, let me see," Max said, ignoring the horns. His eyes were wide again, and he was full of life, the way I liked him best. He grabbed the paper out of my hand. "Yes, yes," he said, "Rockingham Park, yes, yes."

"What's Rockingham Park?"

"It is a track where the horses race. Not far from here."

"I don't get it," I said. I couldn't see why Max was so excited. "Did you win something?"

"Look," he said, thrusting the paper out in front of me. "These are the horses that will race tomorrow night. You see these horses that have circles?"

"Yes." Some of the horses' names had circles drawn in pencil around them.

"B.B. will bet on these horses. These are his picks, you see."

"So?"

"So, don't you see? He will be at the horse track tomorrow night. We will go, you and I, and we will find B.B. You will see."

Horns were still beeping, and people were shouting at Max to get out of the way. Max turned around and shook a fist at them. "Why is it," he said, "everybody is in such a rush?" Then he pulled back into traffic as recklessly as he had pulled out of it.

"Duvid," he said, "you have been to the horse races?"

"No, Grampa."

"Good. You will go. You will enjoy it, you'll see." He seemed happy again.

We drove over the causeway to Plum Island, and for a long time Max was as quiet as before, only now he seemed to be smiling. Sometimes a thought would come to him and his face would get sad again.

I was afraid that something bad was going to happen. What if we went to the racetrack and found the bushy-eyebrowed guy and there was no place for him to run? He might hit Max or something.

"Grampa," I said, "maybe we shouldn't go to the racetrack."

"We must go," he said. "It will be okay. You can bring Kendy if you like."

"It's Candy," I said, "like — "

"Yes, yes, I know, like a Hershey bar," Max said, chuckling.

I felt a little better. If Bushy Eyebrows tried anything with Max, Candy and I could gang up on him.

When we were almost home, I said, "Grampa, what did you mean when you said it could not be B.B. but it was?"

Max glanced at me, as if he weren't going to tell me. Then he looked straight ahead and said, "Duvid, you are confused, but believe me, you are not more confused than your grandfather. I say it was Bernie Bauer because I saw him with my own eyes. I say it could not be Bernie Bauer because Bernie Bauer died forty years ago."

CHAPTER SIX

One thing about being near the ocean is that it really does make you hungry. Ma made pancakes the next morning. I mean pancakes! Stacks and stacks of them, and I gobbled them down as if I hadn't eaten since the third grade.

"You must have a big day planned," Ma said.

"Candy and I are going to play basketball. Then tonight Max is taking me to the horse races. Oh, are you and Nana coming?"

"No. I'm going to bed early tonight."

Ma looked tired. She and Nana and Max had all been sitting in the kitchen late into the night, talking about Max's memories of the old days in Poland with

50

B.B. Max wanted to talk about that stuff because he had seen B.B., or thought he had. I couldn't hear much of what they said, because my room was over the living room, not the kitchen, and the truth is I didn't listen too hard because their talk usually bores me to death. Mostly I just wanted to know about B.B. and how a guy could die in nineteen-forty-something and be running around Newburyport, Masachusetts, forty years later. In fact, I had asked Max that very thing before I went to bed. He had come in to sit on my bed and talk to me the way he always did. But he didn't have much to say when I asked him how B.B. could still be alive.

"As I say, Duvid, it was a different time then," which is what he always said, even though when you think of it, it doesn't really tell you much.

"What are you saying, Max — that people didn't die forever back then?"

Max smiled. "I guess Bernie did not die," he said. "I only thought that he did."

"Well, did you go to the funeral? He was your friend."

"No, Duvid, I did not go to the funeral."

"Was it a heart attack?" I said.

"Don't be silly. Bernie was a young man, and strong like an ox."

"Oh, yeah, I forgot. Then, what? Was it a car crash? Did you see the body?"

"No. I heard that he died. I suppose I heard wrong. Now, *gei schluffen*, go to sleep. Tomorrow we will go to the races and find B.B., and together we can get

51

the whole story right from the horse's mouth? Heh, heh, you get this, Duvid, right from the horse's mouth? At the racetrack!" Max thought this was hilarious. He kissed my head and turned out the light. He was still chuckling when he went out the door.

While I ate my pancakes Max and Nana were still sleeping. I figured maybe Ma could tell me a few things about B.B. When I looked up to ask her, she was hunched over the kitchen counter, staring into a bowl of mashed-up hamburger, peeling an onion, and she had a spoon stuck in her mouth.

"Ma! What are you doing?"

"I aaytn eetow ur unk."

"What? Ma, take the spoon out of your mouth."

She did. "I'm making meat loaf for lunch," she said.

"With a spoon in your mouth?"

"It's for peeling the onion. If you put something metal in your mouth, it stops your eyes from watering."

"No kidding?" I said. "Did an elf tell you that?" I stared at my mother for a long time. She had put that ridiculous spoon back in her mouth. I stared and stared at her and tried to figure out how putting a spoon in your mouth could stop your eyes from watering when you peeled an onion, but I just didn't get it.

"Ma," I finally said, "It's not logical."

"Ut i oo ay?" She took the spoon out of her mouth again. "What did you say?"

"I said it's not logical. I mean, think about it. When you peel an onion, a little spray of onion juice goes flying up to your eyes, and it makes them water. The juice doesn't go anywhere near the spoon in your mouth. The spoon can't possibly stop your eyes from watering."

"David, don't be so logical. Not everything can be figured out with logic." Her eyes were watering pretty heavily, and she wiped them. "Actually," she said, "it doesn't seem to work, but somebody told me it would, and I've just developed the habit."

"Of shoving a spoon into your mouth every time you peel onions?"

"Right," she said.

"Well, while I've got you with the spoon out of your mouth, I want to ask you something. How could a guy who died in 1944 be standing outside an ice cream shop in Newburyport yesterday?"

"You're talking about B.B," she said.

"Yes. I asked Grampa how B.B. died, and he wouldn't tell me anything."

"It was during the Holocaust, honey. Sometimes it's hard for people to talk about that."

I knew that most of Grampa's family had died during the Holocaust, and I had seen a TV movie about the Holocaust, but that was about all. Grampa never talked about that stuff, and Ma and Dad always stopped talking about it when I was around, the same way they did with sex, until they had told me about the birds and the bees — most of which I already knew.

"Well, if B.B. died in the Holocaust, then he couldn't be the guy who was running down State Street yesterday."

"That wasn't B.B.," Ma said.

"Grampa says it was."

"Honey, your grandfather is getting old. Sometimes when people get old, they get sad about the old days and they miss old friends who are gone. And sometimes they get things mixed up, and, well, they see things."

"Are you saying Grampa's crazy?"

"No, of course not. He's not crazy. It's just . . . let's see . . . remember the time your shot from half court brushed against the net at the end of the game and you swore that it went in even though everybody else said it didn't?"

"It did go in."

"It did not, David. And you were obnoxious about it for a week. But anyhow, that's not the point. The point is that sometimes when we want something to be true so badly, we imagine that we see it. Well, that's kind of what happened to your grandfather. He saw that painting the other night and it looked like one of Bernie's and that got Grampa thinking about Bernie. And then he saw that man, who probably looked something like the way B.B. would look and . . . well, it's wishful thinking, that's all."

Ma was probably right. "Poor Max," I said.

"Now, don't go treating your grandfather as if he's sick or something. He's still got the sharpest mind in this family."

"Hey, you don't have to tell me about Max Levene. I'm the guy who discovered him down in the minor leagues. Oh, sure, he was just a young green Jewish rookie then, but I could see that he had potential. Not much of a fastball, but he had a pretty good slider, and as a fielder he was — "

"David!"

"Sorry, Ma, I got carried away. Oh, well, I still want to go to the races, so let's hope Max Levene doesn't figure out that he's only seeing things."

"What's that got to do with it?" Ma asked.

"Max wants to go to the races because he thinks B.B. will be there."

"Oh, dear."

I grabbed my basketball and headed for the door. "And Ma, by the way," I said on my way out, "you know that half-court shot of mine?"

"Yes?"

"It went in," I said. Ma threw a glob of hamburger at me, but I pulled the screen door shut behind me just in time.

Candy was waiting for me in front of the Nautilus sandwich shop. She had a brown paper bag in her hand.

"Sorry I'm late," I said, "but my mother and I were talking about the Holocaust."

I thought I could impress Candy with the big word.

"What about it?" she said.

"Huh?"

"The Holocaust? What were you and your mom saying about it?"

"Oh, come on, Candy, I bet you don't even know what the Holocaust is!"

"Of course I do," she said. "It's when they killed all those Jews. I mean Jewish people. Right?"

So much for my big word. "Right."

"They put them in gas chambers, and giant ovens, millions of them, right?"

"Yeah, yeah, you're right," I said.

"People sure must have been crazy in those days, huh," Candy said. "Want some fudge? My mother made it." She opened the bag and held it in front of me. It was filled with chunks of peanut butter fudge.

"It looks awful, I know," she said, "all crooked and everything, but it tastes good. Have some."

I took some fudge, and we headed for the basketball court.

On the way I told Candy that Max and I had chased some guy down the street. I invited her to come to Rockingham Park with us.

"Of course, we'll have to help Max look for B.B. while we're there," I said, "even though it's not really B.B."

"What if we find him?"

"We'll have to pretend we didn't," I said. "I don't want Max getting into a fight with that guy."

"So, let me see if I've got this right," Candy said. "We're going to look for a guy who's not really the guy we're looking for, and we don't really want to find him, and if we do find him, we're going to pretend we didn't find him. That it?"

"Right," I said.

"That makes sense," she said.

"That makes sense to you?"

"Sure," she said.

"Gee, you're even weirder than I thought."

Candy laughed, and then she said, "There's just one problem. Does it cost money to get in? 'Cause if it does, I don't have any."

"Don't worry," I said. "Max will treat us."

"My father could probably get us in for free if he were around. He trains horses."

"Oh? I thought your father was dead," I said.

"No, David, he's not dead. He lives in California, so I don't see him that much."

"You must miss him a lot."

"Well, of course I miss him," she said, almost as if she were mad at me. "But he and my mother will probably get back together someday. I mean I'm not saying like he'll call us up tomorrow and tell us to come to California, but I bet someday he will."

When we got to the basketball court, there were six kids playing a full-court game. Two of them were about my age, but the others were older.

"The Stingrays," Candy said. "They play here all the time."

"The Stingrays?" I said. "What are they, a motorcycle gang or something?"

"No. That's just what they call themselves, just a bunch of boys who play here in the summer. Some of them live here. The others are just here for the summer, like you."

"Couldn't they just play half-court, so we could play on the other half?"

Candy smiled. "Why don't you ask them?"

"No, thanks," I said. "Maybe if we just stand here, they'll ask us to play."

"Yes," Candy said, "and maybe the sun will turn green. They're never going to ask *us* to play. You, maybe. Not me. They never let girls play."

We watched the game for a long time. There was one kid who was incredible. He was the shortest, but he got more rebounds than anybody. He hit jump shots, hook shots, lay-ups, set shots, even left-handed shots like Larry Bird, and he shot from every-where, and just about every shot went right in . . . *swish*. He could even spin the ball behind his back *twice* on a lay-up.

"That's Larry Cataldo," Candy said. "He plays for Newburyport High. He's good."

"I'll say."

After a half hour it was pretty obvious that Candy was right: The Stingrays were not going to ask us to play. I was sure that if I were taller, they might ask me. But even if they did, they wouldn't ask Candy. So what could I do?

We went back to Candy's house, and she changed into her bathing suit. Then we went to mine, and I got into my bathing suit. Then we went to the beach. Later Ma came over with some meat-loaf sandwiches. Fortunately, she had taken the spoon out of her mouth.

When I got home that afternoon, Max was sitting

out on the deck reading a book about the Vietnam War. I could never figure out why Max read that stuff. His family had died in World War II, so you'd think he'd never want to read anything about war again. I was going to ask him about that when I suddenly remembered that the first time I met Candy she had told me her father was dead and that he had been a war hero. But today she had told me he was a horse trainer in California.

"Why would she lie to me?" I asked Max.

"Who knows?" Max said. "Why did you lie to her?"

"What'cha talking, Max Levene? When did I lie to her?"

"About the dog, Binky," he said.

"Pinky," I said.

"Yes, Pinky. You did not tell her that the dog was following you on the rocks that day, this is right?"

"Oh, that," I said.

"Yes, that," Max said, the way only he can say it.

"Well, because it didn't make any difference," I said. "I mean, the dog was dead, that was the important thing. Pinky wasn't going to come back to life if I told Candy *exactly* what happened. And besides, I just felt, you know, embarrassed."

"Yes," Max said. He patted my shoulder. "I know."

Later we went to pick up Candy for the horse races. Max almost didn't let Candy come because when we got to her house, her mother wasn't there.

"It's okay," Candy explained, "she's never home. She's out tonight."

"And she said it was okay for you to go with Duvid and me to the horse races?" Max asked.

"Oh, sure," Candy said.

"She said this to you? She said, 'Kendy, it is okay for you to go to the horse races with that boy and that old man'?"

"Well, no," Candy said, "I haven't seen her since this morning. But it's okay. I left her a note."

"Hmmn," Max said.

"It's okay, really. She lets me do pretty much what I want. I never get in trouble."

"Hmmn," Max said again. I could see he didn't want Candy to come unless he had talked to her mother, too.

"It's okay, Max," I said. "Besides, we need Candy to help us find B.B."

"Okay," Max said, "but next time, we must talk to your mother."

Rockingham wasn't what I expected. It was better. I guess I thought it would be like Fenway Park. That's where the Red Sox play, and you get an assigned seat and you have to stay in it. At the horse track there are indoor parts where you can sit at tables, and there's an outdoor part where you can sit on benches or just stand around. And you can roam all over the place, which is great if you're a kid, because sitting in one seat for two hours is no fun.

Max took us to the clubhouse, which is a special area above the track. The front is all glass, so you can see the track, which is a giant oval that's over a mile long. In the middle of the oval there's a park with grass and flowers, and a giant scoreboard with a lot of flashing lights that tell you when the next race is starting, what horses are running, and all the things you need to know if you're going to bet on a horse.

Max got us a table with its own little television right in front of the glass. "You can watch the horses on the television, up close," Max said.

It was still about a half hour before the first race, but already there were hundreds of people at the track, walking around and reading the Racing Form so they could decide what horses to bet on.

"I'm going now for a walk," Max said, almost as soon as we sat down, and off he went, clutching the rolled-up copy of the Racing Form that Bushy Eyebrows had dropped when Max was chasing him. As Max walked away I could see him turning his head in all directions, desperately looking for B.B. It made me kind of sad.

"Who's this guy your grandfather is looking for?" Candy said.

"Some guy Max knew when he was a kid in Germany. They used to work together as tailors when they grew up, only the guy was, like, one of the worst tailors in the world," I said. "So he became an artist. Max thinks that one of B.B.'s paintings is in a store in Newburyport, and he's sure that we saw the guy yesterday."

"The man he chased down the street?"

"Right."

"And your grandfather hasn't seen him for a long time?"

"No, see, Max thought B.B. died. But now he says he saw him in Newburyport. My mother says it wasn't B.B. She says Max is imagining things. Anyhow, Max is going to want us to look for this guy, so we'll just walk around and pretend we're looking, okay? That will make Grampa feel better. Then we'll tell him the guy's not here, and he'll probably forget the whole thing in a few days."

"You really love Max, don't you?" Candy said.

"He's all right," I said.

"Oh, come on," Candy said. "You can say it."

"Yeah, I love Max Levene," I said. "He's my buddy."

When Max came back to the table, he looked disappointed, but he forced a smile.

"You shouldn't worry," he said. "We'll find him." Then he looked around at all the people, and he looked out at the track and smiled. "It is good to be here again."

"You've been here before?" I said.

"Certainly. Lots of times." He leaned over and spoke more softly. "Only don't tell Nana. Nana does not always understand about the horses. Better she thinks I was playing pinochle."

"Do you bet on horses, Max?" Candy asked.

"Sometimes," he said. "Come."

Max led Candy and me over to the paddock. That's where they keep the horses.

While we were walking over I asked, "Grampa, are

62

you going to be disappointed if we don't find B.B. here?"

"Yes," he said, "but we will find him before we leave Plum Island. We have nearly two weeks."

"You're going to spend the whole time looking for this guy?"

"Duvid! He was my friend," Max said.

The paddock was a big yard with about ten horse stalls, and that's where the horses that are going to run in the next race walk around so that people can watch them. Max said that some people like to look at a horse before they will bet on him.

Max edged through the crowd at the paddock, so that Candy and I could lean up against the chain-link fence and get a good look at the horses. Candy acted as though she had never seen a horse before in her whole life. She said they were the most beautiful animals she had ever seen. She looked up at Max and waved a finger for him to lean down, as if she were going to tell him a secret. When he leaned over, Candy kissed his cheek.

"Thanks for bringing me here," she said. Max blushed.

After Max stopped blushing, he said, "Now Duvid. And Kendy." He nudged me, so that I would know he was pronouncing "Candy" wrong on purpose. "I have now for you some good tips for betting on the horses." He paused while two big chestnut mares paraded past us.

"Tip number one," Max said. "Do not bet on a horse that limps badly."

Max's eyes twinkled, but he did not smile.

"Oh, you're a riot, Grampa," I said.

"And also do not bet on a horse that sags a great deal when the jockey sits on his back." Candy giggled. "And a horse that falls down quite often, this also is not a good bet." Candy giggled even louder.

"Oh, come on, Grampa," I said, "you must have a system. Everybody has a system."

Max was looking around the paddock area, still hoping to spot B.B.

"A system?" he said. "Yes, yes, I have several systems."

"Great," I said.

"For example, I often use the color system. The program tells me what colors the jockeys are wearing, and I bet on the one that has the most lovely colors. And there is the name system. Let us say a jockey has the same name as someone you went to school with; well, that is a pretty good bet." Still not smiling, Max said, "It is even better if the *horse* has the same name as someone you went to school with. That, Duvid, is a sure thing."

"Grampa! I mean a system that *works*."

"None of them works," Max said. "If they did, how then would the horse track stay in business?"

"What about if you have a lucky number?" Candy asked. "My lucky number is nine."

"Then that is very good," Max said. He glanced around again. "We bet on the nine horse. A thousand dollars."

"A thousand dollars?" I said. "You're going to bet a thousand dollars on a horse?"

"Only make-believe, Duvid, only make-believe. You think I'm crazy?"

We went back to our table. The number nine horse finished last in the first race, and Candy was disappointed. But in the second race, we each pretended to bet ten thousand dollars on different horses. Candy picked a horse named Landfill, because the jockey wore her favorite color, pink, and when her horse won, she jumped up and down and shrieked, "I won, I won," just as if she had bet real money. By the fourth race we were all betting well over a million dollars each.

There's twenty minutes between each race, and Max spent most of the time walking around, staring at faces, hoping to find the man with the bushy eyebrows. After the fourth race he was getting tired and he asked Candy and me to do the searching. He gave us money to get ice cream while we were looking around. At Rockingham they have chocolate and vanilla soft ice cream mixed together.

"Should we really look?" Candy said, after we left Max. "I mean, if this guy isn't even B.B., does that make sense?"

"I don't know if it makes sense," I said, "but we should do it. For Max."

Candy and I walked all over the place. We went to the paddock several times, and we went to the section where rich people have their own tables with their names on them. We went out by the track where there are just a few dozen people until the race begins, and then hundreds of them come out and start jumping and waving their arms and shouting, "Come on, Barbarita," or "Come on, Angel Cake," or "Come on, you stupid nag, I've got ten bucks on you," and things like that. By this time the sun had gone down and the track lights were on, and it was getting chilly out there. Candy and I even snuck into the dining room, where we weren't supposed to be, and took a quick look around.

Every once in a while I'd see a guy I thought was Bushy Eyebrows, and my heart would start thumping. I didn't know what I would do if I found him. I didn't want a fight, and I didn't want to see Grampa chasing some guy around the horse track either. But I also didn't want to have to lie to Max Levene and tell him I didn't see Bushy Eyebrows if I did.

When it was almost time for the last race, Candy and I headed back to the clubhouse. We hadn't seen any sign of Bushy Eyebrows, and I was relieved, but I felt bad for Max. Candy put her arm around my shoulder.

"You're so lucky," she said.

"Me? Why?"

"Because you've got Max Levene. He's great. I mean, the way he goes places with you and everything. I wish I had someone like that."

"What about your mother?" I said.

"Oh, she's okay," Candy said, "but she hardly

ever takes me anyplace. I don't know anybody like Max. I mean, he really loves you, David; I can tell."

"I know," I said, and I could feel myself getting all choked up. Lately I could see that Max was getting old, and I knew I wouldn't have him forever.

"Don't you have people who love you?" I said.

"I don't know," she said. She shrugged, as if it didn't really matter.

After a few minutes, when Candy didn't take her hand off me, I put my arm around her back.

"Candy," I said. "How come you told me your father was dead, and then you told me he was in California?"

I felt her stiffen. "Did I?"

"Yes."

"It must have been a mistake."

"Well, which is it?" I asked.

"Which is what?" she said.

"Which is true? Is your father dead? Was he a war hero like you said? Or is he a horse trainer?"

"David, don't act so stupid. A person can be a war hero and still be a horse trainer, you know."

"Yeah," I said, "but you can't be dead and still be a horse trainer," I said. "They don't allow it."

Candy laughed. "Oh, you!"

"So which is it?" I said.

"Neither," she said, suddenly sounding sad. "My father just left one day, okay?"

"Was he a horse trainer?"

"No," she said quietly, "he was a drunk."

"Is there good money in that?" I said, trying to make her laugh again.

It worked. Candy smiled, and she gave me a big squeeze. "Oh, David," she said, "you're great. I wish you didn't have to go home in two weeks."

"Ten days," I said. "Me, too."

When we got back to the clubhouse and started walking toward the table, we could see Grampa. His elbow was on the table, and his chin was resting on his hand. His head was pressed against the glass. He had fallen asleep.

Candy stopped for a moment.

"Look," she said, "I'm sorry I lied to you about my father. It's just that it's no fun telling people that your father was a drunk who left you and doesn't even call you or anything."

"I understand," I said. "Really." I was thinking it's no fun to tell a girl her dog got killed following you out on the jetty either, but I didn't have the guts now to tell Candy that I had lied.

"I'm not trying to make out like I've had some terrible life or anything," Candy said. "I mean, with my father taking off and all. I know a lot of people have worse stuff than that. But I just want you to know that I think you're real lucky. Your grandfather is super, and I hope you appreciate him."

We woke Max up in time for the last race. We each bet fifteen million dollars. I picked a horse named Short Stuff for obvious reasons. Candy picked Pony Tail because the jockey wore pink. And Max picked a horse named Babbit, because of the two Bs in the name, like B.B. Coming into the backstretch, there were six horses all bunched together, and all three of ours were among them. Half the people at the track were grumbling because their horses were out of the bunch, and the other half were screaming because their horses had a chance. With about twenty lengths to go, Short Stuff pulled away from the group, leaving the others behind, except for Babbit, who came on pretty strong.

"Ugh!" Candy shouted, as Pony Tail started to fade, and all the other horses passed her.

"Come on, Short Stuff, come on, Short Stuff," I hollered. I was jumping up and down. Max was quieter. "Come on, Babbit, come on, boy, you can do it," he said. But it was as if Max was hardly looking at the race. He was staring at the horses, but he seemed to be looking beyond them at something else. With ten lengths to go Babbit pulled up even with Short Stuff, then Short Stuff pulled ahead by a nose, then Babbit took the lead by a head, then Short Stuff closed the gap and the two were even, and with just two lengths left Babbit shot forward one more time and crossed the finish line first.

Candy and I had lost a fortune, but it was great to see Max so happy.

"There, you see," he said. "It was the two Bs that did it. Duvid. Kendy. I always wanted to be a millionaire." He was smiling as we headed for the exit.

When we got outside, everybody was rushing to the cars, hoping to get out of the parking lot before everybody else. But Max just stood in front of the track, forlornly looking around at all the faces of the people who were leaving. Candy and I didn't say anything. We just waited for Max. We stayed there until there was nobody left except the people who worked at Rockingham, and the only car left on the huge parking lot was Max Levene's Buick. The smile had gone from his face, and even as we moved toward the car, Max walked slower than usual, as if there were still a chance that his friend B.B. would come walking out of the building and call to him.

"Don't worry, Grampa," I said. "We'll find B.B." I squeezed his hand, and for the first time I began to think that the man with the bushy eyebrows might really be Max's childhood friend.

CHAPTER SEVEN

If you ever want to see something hilarious, you ought to see Nana in her bathing suit. That's practically the first thing I saw when I got up the next morning. Nana was sitting out on the deck like some beauty queen, wearing this floppy black bathing suit that must have gone out of style back in 1912.

"Good morning, Nana," I said.

"So? Why did you keep your grandfather up to all hours of the night?" she asked.

"What'cha talkin', Nana, it wasn't that late."

"Oh, excuse me, so I'm a liar?" she said.

"No, Nana, you're not a liar."

"Your grandfather is an old man. He can't stay up till the middle of the night like a kid."

"Sorry, Nana," I said. There's no point in arguing with Nana when she gets cranky.

"So," she said, trying to be friendly now, "how much money did your grandfather win betting on the horses?"

"Win?"

"Oh? He lost?" She said.

"No."

Nana smiled. "Good. So how much? How much did he win?"

"In real money?"

"What, is there some other kind?"

"We just pretended we were betting," I said. "We didn't bet any real money. But Grampa won millions on the last race."

Nana looked at me suspiciously. "Don't forget to take out the garbage," she said.

"Right, Nana."

Ma was in the living room ironing a blouse and watching *Good Morning America* on the little portable television we had brought with us.

"Hi, Ma, what's for breakfast?"

"Shh!" Ma lifted one finger in the air. That means "don't talk to me until I finish listening to what the person on TV is talking about." We stood there, both of us listening to the guy on television, and suddenly Nana rushed past us and into the kitchen. Almost as soon as she was out of sight, we heard the sound of cupboard doors being pulled open and the clang of pots and pans being yanked down from shelves and dropped onto the stove.

Ma put her hand to her head. "Oh, God, here we go again," she said. "David, you know you can't say a word like *breakfast* within earshot of your grandmother. Now I've got to go in there and stop her before she cooks herself into a frenzy."

I followed Ma into the kitchen.

Ma, ready for battle, stood in front of the doorway with her hands pressed against her hips. "Mother, what are you doing?"

"A growing boy needs breakfast," Nana said. "I'll just make a few things." She opened the refrigerator and stuck her head and both arms into it.

"Mother, go back to the deck."

"Some scrambled eggs . . ." Nana said.

"Mother," Ma said more forcefully, "you wanted to get some morning sun. This is your chance."

"And some biscuits."

"Mother!"

"The boy must eat," Nana said.

"Yes. *My* boy must eat," Ma said. "But—and I know this is hard for you to believe—I am a grown woman, and I am perfectly capable of making breakfast for my own son."

"Maybe some blintzes. The boy loves my blintzes."

"Mother, get away from that refrigerator right now."

Nana stood up and turned around. She had her

73

arms cradled in front of her, carrying a ton of food. "I don't mind," she said. "I'll be happy to cook the boy a good meal for a change."

Ma's eyes were getting really fiery now, the way they do when Nana pushes her too far. "*I* give 'the boy' . . . *David* . . . a good meal every day. Three times a day, in fact."

Ma might as well have been speaking Swahili. Nana wasn't listening. She began cracking eggs into a bowl and then shuffled a few pans around on the stove.

Suddenly my mother rushed over to the stove and snatched up a frying pan. She held it high in the air as if she were going to clobber Nana over the head with it. Then she slammed it down on the stove.

"Out," Ma shouted, holding the pan over Nana's head again. Nana looked up, squinted at Ma, then started backing away. "Out, out, out," Ma said. "Get away from the stove. Get away from the refrigerator. I don't want to see you in here for the rest of the day."

Nana put up her hands, as if she were in real danger, and she put on this real hurt expression.

"You don't have to ask me twice," she said. "I know when I'm not wanted," and she walked out of the room, making little whimpering sounds the way a dog does when you tie him up in the backyard.

After breakfast Ma said, "Honey, I'm going into Newburyport to do some shopping today. I've got to get out of the house. Nana is driving me nuts. If you and your friend would like to come along, you're welcome."

"Shopping, Ma? I like shopping about as much as I like having a tooth drilled."

"You don't have to stay with me. You can walk around town for a little while."

"A little while? Ma, your shopping trips always go into extra innings."

"Cute," she said. "Real cute."

We had to wait until Candy finished her paper route. Then Ma insisted that we tell Candy's mother where we were going even though Candy explained that she didn't have to get permission. So we drove to the bait shop, which was down at the end of Plum Island where people charter boats for fishing trips. There was a big sign out front that said SHINERS, GRUBS, AND WORMS, and I told Candy it sounded like a law firm, which made her laugh, so I told her some more jokes. I liked it when Candy laughed. Ma and Candy's mother talked practically forever. While we were waiting, I told Candy that I wanted to look for B.B. in Newburyport. I had gotten into the habit of calling the bushy-eyebrowed guy B.B. even though I was almost sure he wasn't B.B.

"Great," she said. "We can pretend we're secret agents."

On the way over to Newburyport, Ma and I took turns telling stories about Nana. Like the time Nana was watching her soap operas and Ma and I were standing out in the rain practically kicking Nana's door down, but Nana didn't even hear us until the commercial came on. By the time Nana came to the door, Ma and I looked like we'd gone swimming with our clothes on, and Nana told us we were a couple of *meshuggenehs* for standing out in the rain. And we told Candy about the way Nana always buys us presents, but when we buy her a present, she acts as though we're trying to have her arrested or something. She can't bring herself just to say thank you. She says, "Ah, what are you buying me a present for? What do I need this for? Don't be such a fool, throwing away your money."

Ma and I also did our impressions. Ma does Nana, and I do Max Levene. By the time we got to Newburyport, we were all howling with laughter over some of the things Nana had done.

After Ma pulled into a parking lot, she turned to Candy in the backseat, and said, "Candy, I hope you realize that David and I both really love my mother. She's a wonderful woman. She'd do anything for you, if you asked her." Ma chuckled. "For that matter, she'd do anything for you even if you didn't ask!"

Then my mother told us about some antiques shops on Merrimack Street she wanted to go to, so she said we should meet her back at the car in an hour. I told her to be realistic. It takes Ma an hour to go through just one antiques shop, so we agreed to meet in two hours instead.

The first place Candy and I went was Annabelle's ice cream shop because that's where Max and I had first seen B.B.

It was still before noon, and Annabelle's was empty. For some weird reason people don't eat much ice cream in the morning. It's always late afternoon or after supper when you have to wait in line. Anyhow, I wasn't interested in ice cream, but Candy and I each got lemonade because it feels stupid to walk into a place and just ask questions without buying anything. After we drank our lemonade, I sauntered over to the counter like I was real cool, and started asking questions. I didn't want the kid behind the counter to think I was real anxious to find out about B.B. I was afraid he might ask me for money the way the informants on television shows always do.

"Say, I'm looking for a friend of mine," I said. "He comes in here sometimes."

"What's his name?"

"His name? Oh, Bernie," I said. "We always call him B.B."

"How old is he?"

"About seventy."

"Seventy?" the kid said. "And he's a friend of yours?"

"Sure," I said. "I have lots of older friends. Anyhow, he's not real tall, about average, and he's got white hair and big white bushy eyebrows. Sometimes he has the Racing Form with him, you know, all rolled up."

"Oh, yeah, I seen him," the kid said. "What about him?"

"I'm looking for him."

The kid peered around the small shop as if there were lots of people there, even though Candy and I were the only customers. Then he looked at me again.

"Well, he ain't here," the kid said.

"Do you know where he lives?"

"No idea," the kid said, and he started swiping the counter with a damp rag as if he were bored with talking to me.

"Well, thanks," I said. As I stepped away I gave him a little wave and accidentally banged my hand against the counter.

As Candy and I were going toward the door the kid called to me, "Hey," he said, "why don't you ask Nettie?"

"Who's Nettie?" I said.

"Oh, nobody. Just the meanest old lady in town. She knows about everything and everybody. There ain't no secrets from Nettie."

"Where do I find her?"

"She's everywhere," he said. "You'll know her when you see her. But be careful. She hates kids like you."

"What do you mean, kids like me?"

"Kids who are still alive!" he said, and he must have thought that was hilarious because he was still roaring with laughter when Candy and I got out on the street.

"This Nettie sounds like a real charmer," I said.

"She's a horror," Candy said. "I've seen her. I always turn and run the other way. Everybody says she was supposed to get married years ago and her boyfriend never came to the church for the wedding, so she got crazy. I don't know if it's true. Some people say she has a dagger in her shopping bag. I heard she can do witchcraft and voodoo, too. You hear a lot of stories. If you want to go find her and ask her about B.B, then I'll wait here."

"No, thanks," I said. "But I appreciate your courage."

Candy jabbed me with an elbow, but not hard.

"Where are we going to look next?" I said.

Candy thought about it. "I've got it! Fowles!" she said, grabbing my hand and tugging me so we could cross State Street. "Yeah, Fowles," she said, as we ran across the street.

"What's a Fowles?" I said.

"It's like a big drugstore that sells cards and candy and paperback books and everything. They have thousands of magazines and newspapers. They must have every magazine in the world."

"So?"

"So, I bet you can't buy the Racing Form just anywhere. B.B. must get it at Fowles."

Fowles was almost right across the street from Annabelle's. It had a big lunch counter on one side, so Candy and I got another round of lemonades, and we had a race to see who could drink the fastest. Candy won. Then we just kind of ambled over to the other side of the store where all the newspapers and magazines were. Candy led me to a stack of racing forms.

"See," she said, "there it is."

While Candy browsed through the fashion magazines I walked up to the guy who stood behind the counter. He was a big fat guy who wore thick glasses. He had a cigar poking out of his mouth, which didn't stink too much, mainly because it wasn't lit.

"So how's business?" I said.

"Pretty good," he said.

"Sell a lot of magazines, huh?" I said.

"A fair amount," the man said.

"What about the Racing Form?" I said. "You sell a lot of them?"

"Some."

"You ever sell one to my friend Bernie Bauer?" I asked. "B.B."

"I don't usually get their names, kid," the guy said. "What's he look like?"

"White hair," I said. "Big bushy eyebrows that look like a couple of shoe brushes."

"This guy any relation to Joe Ballantine?" he asked.

"No. Who's Joe Ballantine?"

"A guy who comes in here. Got the big bushy eyebrows just the way you're describing."

"An old guy? About seventy?"

"Hey, seventy's not so old. I'm sixty-two next month. But, yeah, this guy's around seventy."

"And he buys the Racing Form?"

"Sure does."

"Crap!" I said.

"Huh?"

"Oh, nothing," I said. "Thanks."

I was disappointed. Joe Ballantine must have been the guy Max and I saw. No wonder he ran. I'd run, too, if some old stranger came running out of an ice cream shop and lunged at me like a crazy person. Poor Max, I thought. He was so sure he'd seen B.B., and now I'd have to be the one to tell him that it was some other guy he'd chased down State Street. It was as if I had to tell him all over again that his friend had died.

Candy and I walked up to High Street. She wanted to show me all the fancy old houses. High Street is where all the rich people in Newburyport live, and the houses there are so big you could have a Frisbee tournament inside them. A lot of them have wrought-iron fences, and some have tall columns in front like Greek temples. Most of them have two or three chimneys, and I saw two that had beautiful white banisters on the roof.

Candy knew all the styles of architecture. She pointed out houses to me and told me which ones were Federalist and which ones were Georgian and so on. She explained that you could tell when the houses were built by looking at the architecture.

"Someday I'm going to live in a big house like that," Candy said, pointing to one of the mansions.

"That's the Lord Timothy Dexter house," she said as we passed one huge white house set way back behind a massive lawn. "Someday I'm going to live in a house like that. It's real old. 1771."

"How do you know all this stuff?" I asked.

"I read a lot. History mostly. I think it's good to know a lot."

"You're a regular Max Levene," I said.

"Does Max like to read?"

"Do kangaroos like to hop?" I said. "Yeah, Max reads. He reads books about history." I did my Max Levene impression. " 'Duvid,' he says, 'knowledge is power. You know what I'm talking?' "

As Candy led me down High Street she continued to point out different houses and tell me about the families that had lived in them hundreds of years ago. But my mind drifted. I was feeling sad for Max.

"So Colonel Chase's family must have had a lot of money," Candy was saying, "don't you think so?"

"Huh?"

"David, you're not even listening to me."

"Sorry," I said. "I was just feeling bad. I guess I really thought we'd find B.B."

"I know how you feel," Candy said. "Once I walked all over Newburyport for a whole day, looking for my father. I never thought that he could be in another town or some other state. I was sure he was in Newburyport and that I would find him."

"Did you think you could make him come home?"

"I don't know. Maybe. But even if he didn't come home, I wanted to know where he was and what he was doing. I just figured knowing was better than not knowing. I went into stores and even bars. Nobody had seen him. One man said that if he did see my father, he was going to punch his lights out because my dad owed the guy some money."

Listening to Candy made me glad that I had told her about Pinky drowning, even if I hadn't told her the whole truth. At least she wouldn't have to search all over town looking for her dog.

"I walked around looking for my father until I could hardly stand up anymore, and when I got home that night, I cried and cried," Candy said. "Do you ever cry?"

"Never," I said.

"Well, I do. Especially when I think about my father."

When Candy was little, her father worked at a bank in Boston. He was head teller, and he used to bring her a present almost every night after work. She would sit on his lap, and he would read to her, which was always fun, she said, except when he had liquor on his breath. He used to drink a lot, but he never missed a day of work. She said her father probably could have become an officer of the bank, with a desk of his own.

One summer Candy went to camp in Maine for two weeks, and when she got home, her father wasn't working at the bank anymore. He told Candy and her mother that he had been laid off because they had too many tellers. But he didn't try to get a job at another bank, and they figured something was wrong. He worked as a dishwasher for a while. Then he had a job drilling holes in umbrella handles. He and Candy's mother started fighting. Then he started drinking even more. One night Candy's mother asked him the real reason why he was fired from the bank, and it turned out that he had embezzled money. That means he was stealing, so no other bank would hire him.

He kept getting fired from jobs, and they got into debt and had to sell their house in Boston. Then Candy's father got a job working on a fishing boat off Plum Island in the winter, so they got a cottage to live in because you can rent a place like that cheap in the winter. Candy's father got fired from that job for being drunk, and he started disappearing for a week at a time. Then one day he just left forever. The woman who owned the cottage felt sorry for Candy and her mother, so she said they could rent it all year round for the winter rate. They had been there ever since.

By the time Candy finished telling me all this, we had walked in a big circle all the way back down to the waterfront, where Central Park looks out on the Merrimack River. We cut across the parking lots. Right by the water there is a boardwalk, with benches, and lots of tourists walking around because from there you can look out at all the colorful sailboats. Most of them were anchored out in the middle of the river, but some were sailing along toward the ocean.

Candy and I passed some local artists who sit on stools in the summer and paint pictures of boats on the river, or portraits of tourists. When we came to an empty bench near the place where the tour boat leaves, we sat down. We sat far apart so that both of us could stretch our arms across the top of the bench and tilt our heads toward the sun, which felt good.

"So, I don't know," Candy said. "Maybe my father is dead. I wish I knew."

For a long time we didn't say anything. We just kept our eyes closed and listened to the sounds around us, the tourists talking about Newburyport, the cawing of the sea gulls, and now and then a bell ringing out on one of the boats.

"That's what I don't get about B.B.," Candy said.

"What?"

"About him dying. I mean how can Max not be sure? Either the guy is dead or he isn't."

"Max wasn't there when B.B. died," I said. "Max just heard about it later."

"How did he die?"

"It was the Holocaust."

"Yeah, but, I mean, when exactly, and where? Was it in one of those gas chambers where they killed all the Jews? Yuck. Just the thought of it gives me the creeps."

"I don't know. Max didn't say."

"Didn't you ask?"

"Yeah. But Max doesn't like to talk about those things, because it wasn't just B.B. A lot of his relatives died in the Holocaust, too."

"Concentration camps?"

"Yeah."

"What kind of relatives?" Candy asked. "His mother and father?"

"I'm not sure. A couple of sisters I think."

I felt Candy's hand slide away. She moved closer to me on the bench. I turned, and she looked me in the eye. "David!" she scolded. "What do you mean you're not sure? How can you not know a thing like that?"

"I don't know." I shrugged. "We just never talked about it."

"But these were your aunts."

"No, they weren't," I said. I was annoyed with Candy for being wrong. "They're no relation to me. They were my mother's aunts."

"Well, they're still related to you," Candy said. "Besides, you said you don't know who died. It could have been your great-grandfather and great-grandmother."

"So?"

"So? Well, don't you just wonder about it all? I mean, all those people were killed for no reason, and some of them were relatives of yours." Candy's voice was getting loud. It was embarrassing, because there were other people around.

"It's just not something you talk about," I said. "Besides, it couldn't be for no reason."

"What do you mean?"

"Well, nobody just kills people for no reason," I said. "There had to be a reason."

"Gee, you don't know anything about the Holocaust, do you?" she said.

"I know more than you," I said, "and what the heck are you getting so mad about? You're not the one who's Jewish."

Candy glared at me. "You know, you don't have to be Jewish to think killing people is a horrible thing," she said.

"How would you know anything about being Jewish?" I said, which was a pretty stupid thing to say. I was mad at Candy, but I didn't know why. I stood up. "I'm going to look at paintings," I said. I knew that if we kept talking, I'd just make things worse than they already were.

As I strolled along the boardwalk, looking at the different artists' paintings, I tried not to think about the fight with Candy. Instead, I thought about the lobster painting that Max and I had seen in the store window. Had B.B. painted it? Was it B.B. we had chased down the street? Or was it Joe Ballantine? I started to get excited, thinking maybe Max was right, after all. Maybe it was Bernie Bauer.

Then I glanced across the parking lot and saw something that made me realize how easy it would be to find out for sure. Near the wall of the Fisherman Restaurant there was a phone booth. Of course! How could I have been so stupid? All I had to do was look up Bernie Bauer in the phone book. I started walking toward it. When I got into the open part of the parking lot, I started running. Bernie Bauer, here we come, I thought. I ran harder. It felt good. I knew Max would be proud of me for finding his friend. I ran even faster. When I got to the phone booth, some guy was in it, yakking away. I had to wait. I paced back and forth. I hadn't told Candy where I was going. I hoped she didn't think I just took off because I was mad.

Finally the guy got out of the phone booth. I jumped in and grabbed the Newburyport directory.

"Come on, B.B., be there, be there," I said out loud. People coming out of the restaurant stared at me as if I were crazy. "Bauer, Bauer, Bernie Bauer, be there, Bernie Bauer."

My heart was thumping like mad. I wanted to see that name so badly. It was just like the day at the playground when I had gone to see if my name was on the list of boys who had made the basketball team. And I was just as disappointed when I saw that the name wasn't there. There were Bauers, but no Bernie and no Bernard.

"Damn it," I said. I slammed the phone book shut.

As I walked slowly across the parking lot with my head hanging down I remembered what Ma had told me at breakfast. She had said that Max was thinking about B.B. because of the painting, and he had imagined he saw B.B. because that's what he wanted to see. That was when Ma had used the stupid example about my half-court basketball shot that looked like a swish to me, even though everybody else said it didn't go in. I knew Ma was right. The truth was that the morning after the shot, I knew that if everybody said it didn't go in, then it didn't go in. Of course I wasn't about to admit that, not after all the shouting I did about how everybody except me was either blind or crazy. Poor Max, I thought. Suddenly I felt as if I had been hit by a car, and I went crashing to the ground.

My head was still spinning when I looked up. I had walked into one of those metal grocery carts that people sometimes steal from the supermarket. This one was full of paper bags and empty bottles and junk, and the old lady who had been pushing it was standing over me, screeching, "You rotten little kid, now you've done it, now you've done it." She was real tall and skinny and bony, and she had bags of flesh sagging from her arms the way it hangs from a turkey's neck. Her face was tan and wrinkled like a beat-up old leather bag, and as it came closer to me she stared at me with icy blue eyes. When she got real close to me, her gray hair hung over the front of her face so that it almost touched mine. Her face kept coming closer, and her breath smelled like a roomful of cigarette smoke.

I could feel my veins pounding in my head.

"You have to give me money," she shouted. "You hit my cart. You have to give me money."

She jabbed me three times with her bony fingers. "You people think you can push me around, but you can't. Now you've done it, now you've done it."

This is a nightmare, I told myself; this is a nightmare. But I knew it was real. My skin tingled with fear the way it does when some mad dog comes leaping out of a yard at you while you're bicycling. She poked me some more.

"Cut it out," I cried. "That hurts."

"You bet it hurts," she said. Her voice sounded like something scraping my eardrums. "This will hurt, too," she said. She stood up. I tried to climb to my feet. Suddenly she pushed me with the grocery cart, and I went flying again. While I was down on the ground she banged me with the cart. "Who do you people think you're pushing around?" she said. I tried to get up. *Whack!* The cart hit me again. Finally I jumped away and got to my feet. The old woman got in front of me with the cart, and I backed into a car. I stood there, staring at her, trying to guess which way I should run. She pushed the cart toward me, then she stopped and yanked a bottle out of the cart and tossed it at me. I jumped aside, and the bottle hit the ground and shattered. Then she reached into one of the brown bags and pulled out filthy old rags and threw them at me. "You have to give me money," she said. I turned and ran.

"I'll find out where you live," she shrieked as I dashed across the parking lot. "I'll find out!"

I ran as fast as I could. I knew she couldn't possibly catch up with me, and yet with every step I felt her cold, old claws were closing around my neck. When I'd run almost to the end of the parking lot, I saw Candy rushing toward me.

Candy shouted, "It's okay, she's not chasing you," but I kept running until I landed in Candy's arms.

"Ohmigod," I said, "I was attacked by Nettie. That was Nettie, wasn't it?"

"Yup," Candy said. "That was her."

CHAPTER EIGHT

On Friday morning Max and I decided to go to the beach at the bird sanctuary.

"I hope the car is big enough," Max said. He came out to the porch and handed me some care packages that Nana had prepared. When Nana had found out that we'd be needing a lunch, she was in heaven, and at six o'clock that morning I'd heard her puttering around in the kitchen.

"Pink lemonade," Max said, passing a big jug over the porch railing. I placed it on the floor in the back of the car. "Be careful you don't spill it, Duvid; those pink lemons are hard to find," Max said, chuckling as he walked back into the kitchen. I glanced around nervously, as if Nettie might leap out at me from behind a bush, or maybe come crawling up from the dirt under the cottage. It didn't make sense, but I was still a little bit scared.

When Max came out again, he handed me a basket full of sandwiches and fruit, then a bag of macaroons, some *rugalach* that Nana had baked, and a container of potato salad that was almost as big as a battleship. Nana stood in the doorway, smiling deliriously as we loaded the food into the car.

"I hope that will be enough," she said after I piled the last bag of food onto the backseat.

"I think we've got enough for the first ten days, Nana," I said. "After that we'll send for more."

Nana just smiled. She never laughs at my jokes. I'm not even sure she knows they're jokes. You'd think after living with Max Levene all those years she would know when a person was joking. Still, it was great to have all that food for our picnic, and I wanted Nana to know I appreciated it. I climbed onto the porch and kissed her on the forehead. "Thanks, Nana," I said. Nana beamed.

As Max and I prepared for takeoff Ma came out on the porch to remind us to come back early because my father was driving up for the weekend.

The bird sanctuary is called The Parker River Wildlife Refuge, and it's the main attraction on Plum Island. In fact, most of the island *is* the bird sanctuary. Max and I pulled up in front of the gate. There are guards who count the number of cars that go in and come out, so that nobody can stay there all night. It was a perfect summer morning. The sky looked like a huge lake with little white islands floating across it. Right then I wanted to stay on Plum Island forever.

The gate went up. Max waved to the guard, then we drove along the only road in the sanctuary. I stared out at the miles of grass and marshes and sand dunes. There were no houses, no stores, no pizza restaurants, no buildings of any kind—just open spaces for the birds, and I thought it wouldn't be so bad to be a bird if you could live in a beautiful place like this. I had always wanted to fly, and I could imagine myself soaring through the sky over this sanctuary.

"There, you see," Max said. He pointed to a flock of birds—they looked like some kind of ducks—just sitting around in a marsh. "Nesting. Nobody will bother them."

It seemed to make Max happy, just knowing that the birds could have a place where no one would bother them.

Thinking about Max being happy made me feel edgy because it reminded me that I had to tell him that there was no Bernie Bauer in Newburyport and that the man he had chased was probably Joe Ballantine. When I tried to imagine myself flying again, I couldn't. I just felt sad for Max. So in one second I had turned a beautiful morning into a problem, which is something I do a lot.

After several miles we came to a place where you can park. Max pulled in, and we got all our stuff out of the car. In addition to the sixteen tons of food Nana had packed, we had towels, suntan lotion, books, a portable radio with earphones, my rubber raft, and a beach umbrella. I had even brought my basketball in case there was a basket around, but when I asked Max if there was one, he laughed.

"No," he said. "The birds here do not play besketball. Hockey, yes, but not besketball."

Max was still chuckling about that one as we set off toward the beach with our arms filled with stuff. It was nice to hear him laughing. Maybe I could tell him about B.B. tomorrow, I thought. But I knew I wouldn't wait. I'm terrible with secrets, even bad ones. I always spill my guts, unless it's something like my secret about Candy's dog following me out to the rocks. Those kind of secrets I can keep, at least for a while.

I followed my grandfather through the shrubbery along the winding boardwalk leading to the beach. We were surrounded by bushes with hundreds of red berries dangling from their branches, and if you looked real close, you could sometimes see that on the branches there were birds that blended right in with the colors of the bushes. I could hear and smell the ocean before we got to it. Finally we came over the top of a tall sand dune, and there it was, miles and miles of beach, practically empty.

Max Levene's idea of a good time was to sit on the beach and read a book. So I jammed the beach umbrella into the sand for him and set it up at the right angle so he could be in the shade and still face the ocean.

While we spread out our blanket I told Max about Nettie. When I was all done, Max just said "Hmmn." I think he thought I was exaggerating.

"A bottle, Max," I said. "This . . . this creature threw a bottle at me."

"It is good that you ducked," Max said. He reached into one of the bags for his books.

"Yeah," I said, but Max was hardly listening. I could tell he didn't even believe me. It made me mad, but I figured, okay, I'd just introduce him to Nettie someday and then he'd see.

Max had brought about six books, the way he always did, even though he could only read one. He picked out the one about Jewish people in New York in the early 1900s and as soon as he found his place, he started laughing. Max always said that Jews had the best sense of humor because they had suffered so much, which never made any sense to me. Anyhow, with Max laughing like that I didn't see any point in ruining his day by telling him about B.B., so I went swimming instead.

Off in the distance there were a few people surf-fishing, but, except for them, it was as if Max and I had been stranded on a desert island. The tide was low, so there weren't any great waves, and the water only came up to my waist. The ocean was freezing, but after I got used to it and my body stopped turning blue, I had a lot of fun. I flopped around on my raft. Every time I managed to almost stand up on it, I shouted, "Grampa!" Max would look up and watch

95

proudly as I went tumbling into the water like a flying flounder, then he would smile, wave, and go back to reading his book.

When I came out of the water, Max rubbed suntan lotion all over me. Then he asked me to put the lotion on him, which I thought was a riot since everything except Max's white little toes was in the shade of the umbrella. Then Max read to me from his book. I like to listen to stories.

"Is it lunchtime?" I said when he finished reading.

"Are you hungry?"

"Yes."

"Then it's lunchtime," he said.

The food was delicious, and Grampa and I played a game called Teach Me, where he would teach me something and then I would teach him something. I think about half of what I know is stuff I learned from playing Teach Me with Max Levene. This time he taught me about how cameras work. There wasn't much that Max Levene didn't know, so I usually ended up teaching him something about sports, which was his weak subject. This time I taught him how they keep score in golf because he had never understood why a lower score was better than a higher score. "I don't get it," Max had always said when sportscasters would come on TV and say that Lee Trevino, with a 64, was ahead of Fuzzy Zoeller, who had a 66.

After I explained it to him on the beach, Max said, "Uh. Now I get it."

But then I started explaining about birdies and bogeys and strokes under par, and Grampa stared at me as if I were speaking a language from another galaxy. His tongue came out and sat on his lip, and his eyes got narrow, and he peered at me as if I were trying to pull a trick on him.

"This is golf?" he said.

"Yeah, Grampa."

"Hmmn. You're not trying to fool your grandfather?"

"No, Grampa."

Max thought it over for a few minutes, then he lifted his hands in the air the way he did when he was going to make a major announcement that nobody could deny.

"Golf," he said, "is a *meshuggeneh* game," and that was that. Then he leaned back, opened his book again, and started reading.

I kept nibbling on potato salad and *rugalach*, so that by the time I stopped eating I was too stuffed to go back in the water.

While Grampa read his book I tried to fall asleep, but I kept thinking about Thursday afternoon, and Nettie, and Joe Ballantine, and all that. Finally I couldn't stand it anymore. "Max Levene," I said, "I've got to talk to you."

"Something is troubling you?" Max said as he put his book down.

"Not exactly. But it's going to trouble you."

"Oh?"

97

"That guy we chased the other day. It wasn't B.B. It was a guy name Joe Ballantine, who lives in Newburyport."

Max said nothing.

"See, Candy and I went to this place, Fowles, where they have hundreds of magazines. They sell the Racing Form there, and I talked to the guy behind the counter, and he says this guy Joe Ballantine buys the Racing Form and he's an old guy with big bushy eyebrows, and I figure that's who we chased the other night."

"I see."

"And that's not all," I said. "I checked the Newburyport phone book, and there's no Bernie Bauer."

Max was smiling.

"Max Levene," I said, "what are you smiling about?"

"I am smiling because you make me very happy."

"Happy?"

"Yes, it makes me happy that you would do this for your grandfather, talking to people in stores, looking in phone books. You are a good boy. I am very proud."

"What'cha talkin', proud? I'm telling you it wasn't your friend, B.B., who we saw."

"It was B.B.," Max said.

"Grampa, read my lips. It wasn't B.B. All the evidence —"

"Evidence?" Max said. He pointed to his eyes. "This is evidence." He pointed to his heart. "This is evidence. I know what I see and what I feel. That was

B.B. You wait, Duvid, tomorrow we will go to the art gallery; we will talk to the owner. He will tell us that the painting was painted by Bernie Bauer. You will see. Don't forget the bee."

"Yeah," I said, "but don't you forget that the painting only had one bee, not two the way B.B. always signed his paintings."

"Does not matter," Grampa said, but I could tell that it did matter. Grampa started looking at his book again, but he wasn't really reading.

"So how come you never told me what happened to B.B.?" I said. "What is it, some big secret or something?"

Max glanced up from his book. "No, it's no big secret." He poked me. "Or something. I thought perhaps a boy who is twelve would not be interested in what his grandfather did forty years ago."

Max returned to his book.

"So?" I said.

"So?" Max said, without looking up.

"So, what's the story, Max Levene; you going to tell me or what?"

This time Max closed his book and placed it on the blanket beside him. He sat up and pulled his feet in from the sun. He looked me over, and then he said, "There is not so much to tell. B.B. and I, we ran the tailor shop in Vilna during the years before the war. And when business was not so good, B.B. painted pictures. B.B. and Jacqueline and Klare and your grandfather, we were like the four musketeers, we were always together."

99

"Klare?" I said. "You had a girlfriend before Nana?"

Max smiled. "Duvid, I had a lot of girlfriends before your nana." He stared off toward the ocean and smiled devilishly. "Ah, but Klare? Oh, she was more than a girlfriend; she was my wife."

"Your wife?" I said. The question got caught in my throat. "You were married before?"

"You did not know this?"

"No," I said. My parents had never told me. I felt suddenly as if someone had played a trick on me. "What happened to her?"

"She died."

"Well, how come I didn't know about this?" I said. I hadn't meant to shout, but that's how it came out.

"This was long before you were born."

"Yeah, well I've been around for twelve years now. How come no one's mentioned it?"

Max went on without answering my question. "When the war started and things looked very bad, my mama worried about Klare, because Klare was carrying our baby, and my Klare, well, she was such a gentle person. She would not do well during . . . difficult times. You know what I'm talking? So we sent Klare to America with my sister, Malka. They went to Boston, where we had some relatives."

"Then she didn't die in the war?"

"When the war was over, I came to Boston, to Mattapan. We had an apartment there—me, Klare, and the baby. We could have been happy, but you see, I knew too much of what had happened to Klare's family and my own. I felt always crushed by what I knew. For months I pretended that I did not know where Klare's family from back in Vilna was. I told her we could not find them, and she was full of hope. But, Duvid, you can hold a secret for just so long. One day I had to tell my wife about what had happened in Poland.

"You mean about the Nazis and that stuff?" I asked.

"Yes," Max said. "That stuff. I had watched Klare's mama and papa die, Duvid. And her sisters. The Nazis shot them, as though they were no more than targets. Along with hundreds, thousands of people. There were bodies all over the place. When I told this to my poor Klare, she was never again the same. She became sickly. She cried always. She felt so guilty."

"Guilty?" I said. "What do you mean, guilty? She didn't do anything."

"She survived," Max said. "She went to America. She was safe while her family and thousands of others died. This can make a person feel guilty. And so, my Klare, she died, too. She died from being sick, but I tell you, Duvid, she really died of a broken heart."

"And B.B.?"

"B.B. and Jacqueline returned to Germany before the war. I never saw them again. Many years later when the war was over, I met a man who told me that B.B. and his family had been killed."

"And that's all? You didn't check on it?" I said.

"Duvid, if, God forbid, a friend of yours would die

tomorrow, you would say 'that's unbelievable' and you would ask someone else. You would want to be sure. But in those days, Duvid, if you were told your friend died, it was not unbelievable. You accepted it. Millions of friends died."

I started tapping my fingers on the lemonade jug. I was twitching my neck like mad, the way I do sometimes when I'm trapped in the house on a rainy day and I need to play basketball.

"Yeah, well, never mind about that stuff," I said. "What ever happened to Klare's baby?"

"That is your mother," Max said.

"Ma? I don't get it. Nana is Ma's mother."

"Yes. And she's been a good mother to Ellen for many years. Even before Nana and I got married, Nana took care of Ellen as if she were her own daughter, and when your aunt Nancy was born, the two of them were always treated the same, as sisters should be."

"But if Nana isn't Ma's mother, then she's not my grandmother," I said. I was shouting again, though I didn't mean to.

"Duvid, your nana loves you. She is your grandmother."

"No," I shouted. "It's not the same thing. It's not like a blood relative." I whacked the lemonade pitcher and sent it flying off the blanket.

"Duvid!"

"And why didn't anybody tell me? Don't I have a right to know?"

"It was not for me to tell you. That is for your

102

mother and your father. I thought they must have told you by now. Someday they will tell you."

"When?"

"When they think you are old enough."

"Oh, really, Grampa? Just how old do you have to be to find out that everybody's been lying to you, tell me that?"

Now I was talking so loud, I could hardly hear the sound of the ocean. I stood up and paced in circles. The sand was hot against my feet, and I kicked it.

"You are angry," Max said.

"You're damn right I'm angry," I said. "Everybody I trust has been lying to me. How do I know Ma is really my mother; maybe that's a big lie, too. How do I know anything?"

Max started to say something, but I wasn't listening. I stormed off across the beach, running as if somebody were chasing me.

By the time I calmed down and came back, Max had packed our stuff into the bags. It was time to go. I didn't want to go home yet. I asked Max to drop me off at the basketball court. As we drove out of the bird sanctuary Max asked me to copilot, but I didn't feel like it. When we pulled up in front of the court, I grabbed my basketball out of the backseat. Max put a hand on my knee.

"I'm sorry," he said. "I didn't mean to upset you."

"I'm not upset," I snapped.

"Oh. My mistake."

"Grampa, look at it from my point of view. These people have been lying to me all these years."

"These people?"

"My mother. My father. Nana. Even you."

"Because we did not tell you about Klare?"

"Yes. That's lying, isn't it? Letting me think that Nana was my grandmother."

Max thought about it. "Perhaps you are right. But if your mother and father did not tell you about Klare, I am sure it is because they did not want to tell you about all the things that broke my Klare's heart. They did not want to make you feel sad. Duvid, you cannot imagine the things that went on."

"Grampa! I know all about that stuff; I saw it on television."

"Television," Max said. "I tell you, I wish that I had seen it on television. Duvid, what really happened . . . such things . . . you do not see on television."

I couldn't speak to Max anymore. I didn't want to speak to anybody. So Grampa and I hugged for a long time, then I got out of the car, ran to the court, waved good-bye, and started dribbling my basketball as hard as I could.

I felt real angry. Most of my shots missed and made a loud clang as they bounced off the back of the rim. That just made me angrier, so I bounced the ball harder.

I had been doing this for about fifteen minutes when I heard someone say "You want to play some one-on-one?"

I turned around, and I couldn't believe what I saw. It was Larry Cataldo, the kid who played for Newburyport High. He was standing on the court, in shorts and a T-shirt, with a basketball under his arm. He had come down to shoot around, and there he was asking *me* if I wanted to play one-on-one. That was like the Boston Celtics calling up the local Cub Scout troop and saying, "Hey, you fellows want to scrimmage with us?"

"Who me?" I asked, even though there wasn't anybody else around.

"Sure. We'll play to twenty-one by ones. I'll spot you ten points."

"I've seen you play," I said. "I think you should spot me twenty points and let me take the ball off first."

He smiled. "Well, let's see if I can beat you with ten first, then we'll talk about giving you a bigger lead." He came over and shook my hand. "Larry Cataldo," he said.

"I know," I said.

"Huh?"

"I mean, uh, David Newman."

We played half-court basketball. Larry was short for a high school basketball player, but he was a lot taller than me and he was real muscular, especially in the shoulders. He could have moved close to the basket and just tossed the ball in every time if he'd wanted to. But he didn't do that. He shot mostly jump shots from outside, and now and then a fancy lay-up. But it didn't matter. All of his shots went in.

When I got the ball, I played like a maniac, partly

because I was still mad at my mother and my father and pretty much the whole world, and partly, I guess, because I wanted to impress Larry Cataldo. I ran as fast as I could, and dribbled as hard as I could, and jumped as high as I could. It felt great. Larry was a little cooler than all that. He just kind of danced with the ball, dribbling circles around me, and we both knew he could pop it in the basket pretty much anytime he felt like it. I couldn't believe I was actually playing with this kid. He must have been sixteen years old, maybe seventeen.

By the time I got my first basket, he had gotten seven. With the ten points he gave me at the start, I was still ahead eleven to seven. Larry was murder on the boards. But I didn't give up. I went up for every rebound, just as if I really had a chance, and I did pick off a couple of rebounds. After one of them I dribbled out to the foul line, faked left, ran right, and laid it in.

"Great move," Larry said. I couldn't believe it . . . Larry Cataldo saying "great move" to me.

By the time Larry had twenty baskets, I had gotten five and was up to fifteen points. He could have shot one in and ended the game at any time, but I think he deliberately missed a few shots so I'd have a chance to score some more baskets. After a while he started talking to me when I had the ball, as if he were my coach calling out instructions from the sideline. I shot one and missed.

"You missed because you were looking at me," he said. "You were worried about getting fouled. Once you've decided to shoot, don't look at the defensive man. Look at the basket."

After Larry pulled down the rebound, I stole the ball, though I think he let me, and I shot again. This time I looked only at the basket. It went in.

"Perfect," he said.

When I got up to seventeen, I guess Larry decided to finish me off. He dribbled out to almost half court. I ran out to guard him.

"Don't cover a man this far out unless you think he can put it in from here," he said. "Otherwise you're just wasting your defense."

"Oh," I said, and I pulled back about six feet. Then from half court he leapt in the air and let the ball fly. It went in. *Swish*. He smiled at me. "Now you know," he said.

Larry wanted to play another game, but I knew I had to get home because my father would be there waiting to see me.

"You really play hard," he said. "You could be a real good player."

"If I were taller," I said.

"You don't have to be tall to be a good basketball player," he said. "Did you ever hear of Spud Webb?"

"Well, yeah," I said. "Atlanta Hawks. Five foot seven." I was showing off my knowledge of professional basketball, but actually I felt like an idiot because "Did you ever hear of Spud Webb?" was what I always said when other kids told me I was too short to play. "Do you think someone my height can make a high school team?"

"What grade are you in?"

"I'm going into the eighth."

Larry smiled. "When I was in the eighth grade, I was about as tall as you are now. And it was murder. Nobody wanted me to play on their team. They figured I'd get my shots blocked or that I couldn't play defense against taller guys. I hated that."

"Right," I said. "That's exactly how it is." I couldn't believe Larry Cataldo and I had something in common.

"I used to think, 'Someday I'll show those big guys'."

"Right," I said. "That's what I want to do." It was as if he were reading my mind. "So what did you do?"

"I learned not to play as if I were tall."

"What do you mean?"

"Well," he said, "us short guys have got to play our own game. You can't let the tall guys force you into their game. Tell you what, you come down here some day when you've got time, and I'll teach you what I mean."

I couldn't believe it. Larry Cataldo was going to teach me some basketball.

"Really?" I said.

"Really," he said. "Us short guys, we've got to stick together."

Things were definitely looking up. Maybe he would be my friend. Basketball, I thought. This is why the chief elf sent me to Plum Island.

As I walked back to the cottage I decided I would

spend the rest of my vacation playing basketball. Maybe Larry would teach Candy, too. The heck with B.B., I told myself. If my family didn't want me to know about all that other stuff, that was just fine with me. It was creepy anyhow, so the heck with them, I just wouldn't ask. They could stay up at night talking about B.B. as much as they wanted. I would spend my time learning to play basketball like a pro.

CHAPTER NINE

On Sunday morning I was still pretty annoyed with my parents for not telling me about Klare and Nana. But I didn't say anything. We were all, including Candy, going to the Salisbury Beach amusement park, and I didn't want to be the one to spoil everything by bringing up the fact that they were a bunch of liars. And besides, I had decided that if they didn't want to talk about that stuff, then neither did I.

At quarter to ten my father stood in the living room and announced, "The train leaves at ten o'clock. Anybody who's not aboard will be left behind." That's what he always says when he wants us to be in the car by a certain time. He expects people to take him seriously, even though he's never actually left anybody behind.

We all got in the station wagon. Ma and my father were in the front. Max and Nana were in the backseat, and Candy and I were way in back so we could face out the rear window and have our own conversation.

"What's wrong with your grandmother?" Candy whispered in my ear as we pulled out from the cottage.

"Nothing, why?"

"You keep staring at her," Candy said.

"Oh." I hadn't realized it, but Candy was right. I was staring at Nana, trying to figure out who she was if she wasn't my grandmother. "I'll explain it later," I said.

Salisbury Beach is near the New Hampshire border. It's on the ocean, so there are miles of beach as well as the amusement park, and the whole area is filled with race car places, fried dough stands, water slides, miniature golf, and all the other things that make life worth living. To get there, we had to go over the bridge from Plum Island into Newburyport.

"We must stop in Newburyport," Max said as we crossed the bridge. Candy and I were counting sailboats.

"Pop, what for?" my mother asked.

"It is Sunday," Max said. "The owner of the art gallery will be there. Now we will all find out that Bernie Bauer painted that picture."

"Oh, Pop," Ma said. "Why do you want to go and

upset yourself. B.B. is dead, and you're just . . . seeing things."

"You will see things," Max said. "You will see that B.B. painted that picture."

Ma turned to him. "Pop, you said yourself that the painting only has one bee. And David found out that the man you chased was not B.B."

Max wasn't about to give in. "The man was B.B.," he said. "Max Levene you don't fool."

My mother and father gave each other a look, as if to say Poor Max, he's gone crackers. I felt bad when I saw that. I was sure the man we chased wasn't B.B., but I was also sure that Grampa wasn't crazy.

"Okay, we'll stop," my mother said, "but I hope this will bring you to your senses. This B.B. thing has got all of us upset."

When we got to Newburyport, the only parking spot was across the street from the art gallery. Sunday is real busy in Newburyport because a lot of people come up for the weekend. When Dad pulled up to the curb, Max got out and began walking across State Street while we all waited in the car. I watched Max. He was walking more slowly than ever, and stooping slightly, as if he were carrying something heavy on his back. He looked kind of pitiful. I pushed the back hatch open and jumped out. "I'm going with Grampa," I said, and I ran to catch up with him.

Inside the art gallery we saw the same woman Max had talked to, the one Max had called a *schlemiel*. We asked for the owner, and a tall, thin guy came out. He was smiling and rubbing his hands together as

112

if he expected to sell us a ten-thousand-dollar painting.

"Yes, may I help you?"

Max took him to the window and pointed to the lobster painting.

"You know the man who painted this?"

"Certainly. His name is Hooley Fuller."

"Hooley?" Max said. His eyes darted back and forth suspiciously. "What kind of a name is Hooley? It sounds to me like a made-up name."

"Well, that's his name," the owner said. "Are you interested in this painting?"

"Yes, I'm very interested," Max said. "This man, Hooley, he is about my age?"

The owner looked at Max. "Oh, no. Not at all. Hooley? Oh, I guess he's about thirty."

"No," Max insisted. "This cannot be."

"Well, I believe I'm right," the man said. He called to the *schlemiel* woman. "Hooley Fuller? Wouldn't you say he's about thirty?"

"About that," she said.

Max pointed to the painting once more. "The man who painted this painting, with the bee?"

"Yes," the owner said. He pulled the painting out of the window and put it into Max's hands.

"Hooley does very good work. He always signs with a bee."

"Hmmn," Max said.

"Possibly we can let this one go for four hundred if you are interested," the man said.

Max didn't answer. He just stared off into space,

and he held the painting for a long time, as if he didn't want to let it go.

Finally the man took the painting from Max's hands and placed it back in the window. "Hmmn," Max said again, and he walked slowly to the door.

When we got back in the car, Ma asked Max what had happened, but he didn't answer. He just stared out the window of the car.

"The painting was by some thirty-year-old guy," I said, "not B.B.," and all of us were quiet for a while.

On the way to Salisbury Beach, Candy and I spent the time spotting cars. She had Toyotas and I had Subarus. The deal was if I found more Subarus and won, she had to go on the roller coaster with me, and if she won, I had to go on the merry-go-round with her and actually ride on one of those dumb horses that go up and down. Fortunately, I won.

By the time we got close to the amusement park, Max didn't seem so sad. It seemed as though he had finally accepted the fact that B.B. did not paint the lobster picture.

"Hey, Max Levene, did you see any *mahooblishehs* on the highway?" I said, figuring I'd find out what kind of a mood he was in.

"Yes, Duvid, I saw three of them. I would have said something, but I didn't want to disturb you."

"I see," I said. "Are you going on the roller coaster with me?" I said.

Max turned around and gave me a look.

"I would love to, Duvid, but not today."

114

"Oh?" I said. "You wouldn't be afraid of the roller coaster, by any chance, would you, Max?"

"To tell you the truth, Duvid, I go on so many roller coasters, I get sick of them. You know what I'm saying?"

"Really, Max? Tell me, when was the last time you were on a roller coaster?"

"Funny you should ask. Why, just yesterday I was on three of them. So it's not surprising that I would not feel like going on one today."

"Yesterday, huh?"

"Yes, yesterday, while you were playing besketball."

"Basketball, Max, basketball," I said.

"Yes, that's what I said, besketball," Max said, and he gave Candy a wink because he thought he was putting one over on me.

When we got to the amusement park, my father told Candy and me to stay with the grown-ups for a while. "Family time," he called it, even though it was pretty obvious that Candy and I wanted to do some things that didn't exactly excite Max and Nana and my mother and father. Like ride the water slide, for example. So, for a long time we walked around like old people, stuffing our faces with cotton candy.

The amusement park had a lot of games like the ones you see at a carnival, but most of them were stupid. My father won a doll for my mother by knocking down milk bottles with a baseball three times straight. So I tried to win one, too, but instead I won the fool of the year award by missing the bottles all three times. Plus, I practically clobbered a woman behind me when I wound up too fast for the third pitch and sent the ball flying in the wrong direction. After that I got us to the basketball shooting game as quickly as possible, figuring I could make a comeback by winning a doll for my mother. I got four out of five baskets, but the prize was just a dumb purple comb that was about as big as a garden rake.

Finally, Dad said Candy and I qualified for his "early release program" because we had been "model prisoners" and we could go off on our own as long as we checked in with him every forty-five minutes.

First Candy and I went on the water slide, which was incredible. We had to get into our bathing suits, then climb hundreds of stairs up a tower that was so high, we could see all the way to Newburyport. But it was worth it. The slide has water constantly flowing down it, and we went zooming down like a couple of Indy 500 racers. The slide turns in all different directions. It was a riot. We shrieked all the way even though the slide isn't really scary, except for the first couple of times when you go flying around a curve and feel as if you're going to be shot into orbit.

After we had climbed the stairs and gone down the slide about ten times, Candy and I were getting exhausted, so we got dressed and went on the roller coaster.

Once we had done that, I went on the merry-go-round with Candy, even though I didn't have to. I thought doing that would make her happy, but if you didn't know, you'd think that somebody had forced her to ride on the merry-go-round. She didn't smile once all the time she was bobbing up and down on the pink wooden horse.

As we climbed down from those ridiculous horses I looked around. I wanted to be sure nobody from Westbridge happened to be at Salisbury Beach that day watching me ride on a merry-go-round like some five-year-old. Then I asked Candy if she wanted to go on the Ferris wheel.

"Sure," she said, but she said it as if she had a toothache or something.

A few minutes later we were stuck at the top of the Ferris wheel so they could let other people on. The people and the rides down below us looked like parts to a model train set, and way out on the ocean I could see tankers. I pointed things out to Candy, but she just nodded. I asked her what was wrong.

"I miss Pinky," she said. "The last time I was here, Pinky was with me."

"Oh," I said. I felt uncomfortable. "You haven't talked about her, so I didn't bring it up," I said.

"I know. I've been thinking about Pinky all the time. But I was afraid to talk about her."

"Why?"

"Because I knew I'd cry," Candy said, and right away the tears started to flow down her cheeks. She pulled a tissue out of her jeans.

"I haven't talked about her because I thought it

117

would make you feel sad," I said. But I knew that was only part of the reason. "Do you want to talk about Pinky?"

Candy nodded.

"Tell me some of the good stuff," I said. "Like, when did you get Pinky?"

Candy's mother had seen an ad in the newspaper for Labrador pups and had bought one for Candy's eleventh birthday.

"Pinky was so shy when we first got her, but then she got playful," Candy said, smiling through her tears. "She chewed on shoes all the time—sneakers, slippers, it didn't matter, as long as it was something you wear on your feet. She used to chew on a shoe and get it all wet with dog spit, and then she'd bring it to me to play. Yuck, it was disgusting! My mother always said that Pinky had been a shoe salesman in a previous life. After a while I trained her to only chew on the old shoes we gave her as toys.

"When she got bigger, she went everywhere with me. People called us Mutt and Jeff because we were always together. But sometimes when I left Pinky in the yard, she would wander off, the way she did the day you saw her. I tried to block all the holes in the fence, but she always found a way to get out!"

Finally, the Ferris wheel was turning. Candy kept talking about Pinky. It was like music, the way she described her dog's antics. But all the time she was talking I felt something scary building up inside me, as if I were getting closer and closer to a dentist's appointment. It was guilt, I guess, because I hadn't told

118

Candy the whole truth about how Pinky died. I felt kind of trapped up there on the Ferris wheel. It would have been nice if I could have told Candy the truth and then run away, but I wasn't about to jump out of the Ferris wheel. And I knew I had to tell her. It just wasn't right not to.

By the time the Ferris wheel stopped spinning, Candy was smiling again.

"I've got pictures of Pinky," she said. "Lots of them." She wiped the last tears from her eyes. Now we were trapped at the top while they let people off. "Thanks, David."

"For what?" I said, though I guess I knew.

"For listening to me. I feel much better just talking about it."

"Good," I said, though I felt much worse myself. I wanted to tell Candy the truth so I wouldn't have to feel like a skunk anymore, and I wanted to tell her before we got off the Ferris wheel, because I knew I'd lose my courage if I let too much time go by. The Ferris wheel moved forward, and we went down one spot. I braced myself.

"I have to tell you something," I said.

"What?"

"It's about Pinky."

Candy looked at me strangely; then I realized she might get some crazy idea that I was going to say something really bizarre, like "Pinky's not dead" or something, so I just blurted it out.

"When I saw Pinky fall off the rocks, it wasn't exactly the way I told you. Pinky was following me. If

I hadn't gone out on the rocks like a big shot, she wouldn't have been there, and she'd probably still be alive. So it's partly my fault that she died."

There. I had said it. I felt better. Lots better. But my heart was thumping. I thought something awful was going to happen. Candy would accuse me of killing her dog. "Murderer, Murderer," she would shriek from the top of the Ferris wheel, and everybody in the amusement park would gawk up at us as if we had escaped from a mental hospital. Or Candy would cry something awful, and I wouldn't know how to handle it. Or she'd get hysterical and start punching me and trying to push me out of the Ferris wheel.

But it wasn't like that. Candy was real quiet, and after a minute she said, "It's not your fault, David. Pinky was always following people." And that was all. It was so easy, I wished I had told her a long time before.

When I was sure Candy was okay about Pinky, I said, "Look, since we're spilling our guts here, there's something else I want to tell you. I found out Friday that my grandmother isn't really my grandmother."

I told Candy all about my conversation with Max at the bird sanctuary, and when I finished, she asked me what it was like to be Jewish. I didn't really have a good answer, but I described the holidays and going to temple and my bar mitzvah, which I'd have to get ready for as soon as school started. Then for a while we talked about what it was like not to be Jewish. After that we talked some more about her father, and my brother, Markie, who was at music camp. Then

Candy told me that she had always wished she had a little sister. I told her how crummy I had felt when I found out I was left off the basketball team. I asked her if she had ever felt that way. She said that she had once tried to run away to Nebraska when she got two D warnings in the same marking period but had only gotten as far as Fowles, where she had a soda and then went home.

By the time we were driving home, Candy and I had told each other practically everything that had ever happened to us. All that talking felt great. But the more I thought about how good it felt to talk and how lousy it felt to hold things in, the more I realized that I had to tell my parents I was angry because they had lied to me about Nana, and hadn't even told me about Klare.

That night the family cooked out on the grill. Actually, Dad did the cooking. Ma announced that she was on strike, which she does every once in a while when she is sick of housework. I helped by carrying out the hamburgers and mustard and salad and all that while Ma stretched out on a lawn chair. She said things like, "Oh, this is wonderful, watching you gentlemen prepare supper," and "Don't forget to shake the salad dressing."

After we ate, Nana and Max sat out on the deck the way they did every night. They liked to stare out at the water, where people paddled canoes or floated on rubber rafts, because there were no waves. Ma and Dad went into the kitchen and started putting things away. Ma is like that. Even when she goes on strike, she can't bear the thought of me and Dad putting kitchen things away, because she's afraid she'll never see them again. I grabbed the bag of charcoal and followed them into the kitchen. I knew Dad would be driving back to Westbridge, so I had to talk to them now, or hold it in for another week.

I was nervous. "So, Ma, Dad," I said cheerfully, "told any good lies lately?"

They both smiled. "What do you mean?" my mother said.

"Oh, I don't know; I mean, about, like people's grandparents, things like that?"

"Something on your mind, David?" my father asked.

"I know about Klare," I said.

They looked at each other.

"Who told you?" my father asked.

"Max Levene," I said. "You guys sure never did. I guess you don't think a kid has a right to know who his grandmother is. Or who isn't."

"Oh, David," Ma said.

"Never mind 'oh, David,' " I said. "You've been lying to me for years, making a fool out of me."

"David!" my father said. "I know you're hurt, but that is not an appropriate way to talk to your mother."

"If she is my mother," I muttered.

"What was that?"

"I said, 'if she is my mother.' How do I know? You lied to me about Nana. You could be lying to me about anything. Maybe you found me in a Laundromat or something. I could be from Nebraska or even Delaware. Maybe I'm not even Jewish. How would I know? I can't trust you people to tell me the truth."

"Oh, honey," Ma said. "We were going to tell you."

"When? When I'm fifty?"

"We thought perhaps after your bar mitzvah. Next year."

The last thing I expected was that I would start crying over this thing. But that's what happened. Before I could even stop them, there were tears in my eyes and my throat felt as if someone had shoved a paper towel down it.

"Well, I should have been told," I said. "I should have been included. All these years I've been treating Nana as if she were my grandmother, and she's not my grandmother. She's just some woman Max married after his wife died."

"Nana is your grandmother," my father said. He came around the kitchen table to where I was standing, and put his hands on my shoulders. "She's been everything a grandmother should be. And what if you had known? How would you have treated her differently?"

"I don't know," I said. "It's confusing."

"I know it is, son. But she's as much of a grandmother to you as Klare would have been. Nothing's different."

I grabbed a napkin from the table and wiped my eyes. "If nothing's different," I said, "then why keep it a big secret?"

Ma pulled out one of the chairs at the table, and she sat down. Her face looked tired.

"Did Grampa tell you why my mother died?" she said.

"He said she had a broken heart."

"She did. She died of pneumonia. But what really killed her was the sadness she felt. When my father came here from Europe and told her what had happened to her family, she was never the same again. I was just a little girl, but I have such strong memories of my mother crying every night. She would ask God why He had done this terrible thing. She was so miserable, it was unbearable. David, that is the worst thing that ever happened to me, watching my mother slowly disappear from my life until she died. Don't blame your father for this. He wanted to tell you a long time ago. I was the one who didn't want to tell you, because there was no way to explain it without telling you about all the horrible things that had happened to my mother's family and to Grampa."

"You mean the Holocaust," I said.

"Yes."

"I already know about that."

"No, David, I don't think you do."

"I know about the Nazis. That they had death camps. And they killed Jews."

"And what else?" my mother said. I felt my father's hands pressing gently on my shoulders.

"What do you mean, what else?" I said.

"What else do you know?"

"That's it," I said. "What else is there to know?"

"Honey, sit down." I sat down at the table. My father pulled out a chair, and he sat next to me. Ma looked into her hands for a while, and then she looked into my eyes. She turned and glanced toward the living room.

"I have to speak quietly," she said. "I don't want to upset Max."

She picked up a spoon that was on the table and started playing with it while she spoke, which is what she does when she's tense.

"Honey, before World War Two there were millions of Jews in Europe. It wasn't like Westbridge, where we are practically the only Jewish people. When Hitler took over Germany, the Nazis forced Jews to live in ghettos. Hitler had been blaming the Jews for Germany's economic problems, and his plan was to kill every Jew in Europe. He put them in concentration camps where they were prisoners. They were forced to work and had almost nothing to eat. He built gas chambers. He killed six million Jews."

"I don't understand how it could happen," I said.

My mother reached across the table and took my hand. "Of course you don't. We don't understand it either. Nobody understands that kind of hate. It's too monstrous to understand. If you and I and Dad and Markie had lived in Germany at the time, we would have been killed, all of us. For being Jewish."

My mother looked at my father to see if there was anything else to say. Dad didn't speak. He just patted my shoulders again, maybe to remind me that I was safe.

"And it wasn't just Germany," my mother continued. "The Nazis murdered Jews in other countries. When they invaded Poland, they killed three million Jews there. Max was taken to one of the concentration camps."

It was a frightening picture in my mind, Max Levene being taken away in handcuffs by a bunch of Nazis. I pictured him the way I knew him, as an old guy, even though I knew he was much younger in those days.

"Which one?" I said. I had heard of Auschwitz and Dachau, and I knew there were others. Suddenly it seemed important to know exactly what had happened to Max.

"Huh?"

"Which one? Which concentration camp was he in?"

"Well, I don't know. It was in Poland. He was in several of them."

"Did they have handcuffs then?"

"What do you mean?"

"When they arrested Max, did they use handcuffs?"

"I don't know," Ma said.

"How long was he in the concentration camp?"

"Three years I think." She turned to my father. "Maybe it was four years. What's the difference?"

"What did he eat?"

"David, what kind of a question is that? I don't know what he ate. Just scraps, I guess. It doesn't matter."

126

"I bet it matters to Grampa," I said. "Did he have a bed to sleep on?"

"David," my mother said firmly. "I don't know."

"Didn't you ever ask?" I could feel myself getting angry. But it wasn't my mother I was angry at. At least, it wasn't only her. It was more as if I were angry at everybody, including myself.

"Well, no. It's not the kind of thing you ask."

"Why not?"

Now my father spoke. "David, don't you understand, your grandfather went through terrible things that we can hardly even imagine. He doesn't want to talk about something like that."

"I bet he does," I said.

"David, lower your voice. You're shouting."

"I'm going to ask him. I'm going to ask him what he ate and if he had a bed."

"David, I don't want you dredging up all that stuff with your grandfather. He doesn't want to talk about all the pain he went through."

"Ma, you always said that I know Max Levene better than anybody. And you know what I think? I think it's painful for him not to talk about it. He probably thinks nobody wants to hear about it. And he's right. But he's not right anymore. *I* want to hear about it."

"David," my father said, "your mother has spoken. You are not to bring this up with your grandfather. Do you understand?"

"No, I don't understand," I snapped. "I'm going to play basketball." I had to get out of the house. My whole body was twitching.

"Promise me you won't talk to Max about this," my mother said as I headed for the stairs.

"I can't promise, Ma," I said. "I have to think about it. I'm confused."

I went upstairs and got my basketball. When I came back through the kitchen, my mother and father were still talking about it.

My mother said to me, "You have to understand that your grandfather is an old man. He's put all that stuff behind him. If you bring it up, you'll just make him terribly sad. Believe me."

"If he's put all that stuff behind him, Ma, then why is he imagining that he saw B.B.?"

"I don't know," my mother said. "I just don't know."

CHAPTER TEN

When I got to the basketball court that night, Larry Cataldo and three Stingrays were playing.

I watched the Stingrays play for a while. They could all shoot from outside better than I could, even though I'm a good outside shooter. They could hit jump shots and lay-ups. They could even pass without looking at the guy they were passing to. Of course they were all older than me, but I was beginning to wonder if I would ever be that good.

I was still kind of shaken up from my conversation with my parents and I needed exercise, so I went to the other basket and started dribbling and shooting. Sometimes when I play basketball I pretend I'm

Danny Ainge or Isiah Thomas, or even Spud Webb if I'm feeling real small. This time I pretended I was Larry Cataldo. I tried to dribble like him and double-pump the ball on lay-ups the way he would. But it was a lot harder than it looked. A couple of times I accidentally smacked myself in the face with the basketball. After a while I just went back to being me. Every time I popped a shot in, I turned around to see if Larry had noticed. Sometimes he did. I shot pretty well, even though I was thinking about Grampa and the Holocaust and all that.

Poor Max, I thought. My parents were wrong, I was sure. Max probably wanted to talk about the Holocaust. I know what it is like when you don't have anybody to talk to. I decided I'd ask him to go fishing and then we could talk about it all.

Max Levene, I thought. I walked out about fifteen feet and started shooting one-handed set shots, trying to get one in for every letter of Max's name. *M*, I thought, and took a shot. *Swish*, it went in. *A. Swish. X. Swish.* Then I missed the *L* and the *E*, but I got *V*, *E*, and *N* before I missed the third *E*. Thinking about Max made me smile.

"That's twenty-one, you bozos," I heard Larry shout, and I knew the game was over. The other three kids left, and Larry stayed down at the other end of the court shooting around.

I kept shooting and dribbling and thinking about Max and the Holocaust. Then I heard Larry Cataldo behind me.

130

"You want to play basketball with the Stingrays?" he asked.

I gulped. "Me?"

"Sure."

"Play with the Stingrays?"

"Do you want to?"

"When?"

"I don't know," he said. "Sometime."

"Yeah, that would be great, except I'll probably look like a total fool."

"Don't worry about it. You and I will play Tony and Pinch, the two guys I was just playing against. The short guys against the tall guys. There's just one thing."

"What's that?"

He smiled. "I want to beat those bozos."

"Oy!" I said.

"No problem," Larry told me. "You've got a good outside shot. We've just got to deal with the height problem."

"You mean my being short?"

"No," he said. "Them being tall."

First Larry showed me that I didn't have to be tall to get my share of rebounds. "Position is more important than height," he said. He showed me how to get in position to grab rebounds and how to spread myself wide to block out the defensive man. He told me to lean forward and stick out my butt, so that the man behind me would have to lean forward to try to snatch a rebound away from me. That would throw him off balance.

"Okay," Larry said, handing me the ball after we did some rebounding drills, "now take a hook shot on me."

I swung around in the pivot and took a right-handed hook. Larry blocked it.

"Again," he said.

I shot again. He blocked it again. I shot a third time. He blocked it a third time.

"What's the problem?" he said.

"My height," I said, and Larry nodded.

"Now swing around the same way, and fake the shot. Don't lose control of the ball. Then swing back to your right. You won't be able to shoot it over me there, either, but my arms will be way up high to block the shot, and you can scoop it under me. You don't need height to do that."

We went through the shot slowly. Fake left, swing right, scoop under. Fake left, swing right, scoop under. Fake left, swing right, scoop under. Finally I got the rhythm right, and a miracle happened right there on Plum Island. The ball went in. I had scored in the pivot with a taller man guarding me. It was one of the great moments of my life.

"Great," Larry said. "Now do it ten more times."

I did it ten more times, and the ball went in five of them.

Then Larry showed me what would happen if he dropped his hands to block the scoop shot. It left the basket wide open, with me only a few feet away. An easy jump shot off the backboard. I was beginning to realize that being short wasn't the end of the world, basketballwise.

Next Larry showed me how to set a pick.

"You don't have to be tall for that either," he said. "When you set a pick, you're acting as a barrier between the shooter on your team and the man who's trying to guard him. The defensive man can't walk through you, so it doesn't matter how tall you are."

Then Larry taught me the give-and-go, the reverse lay-up, and the behind-the-back pass.

We played until it was almost dark. I didn't want to leave. I started *kvetching* that they should have lights on the court so people could play basketball all night if they wanted to. Larry just laughed at me. "Go home," he said. "We'll play again tomorrow."

The next morning Max and I left the cottage to go fishing. I was still thinking about the Holocaust, but what I talked about was basketball and all the things Larry had taught me.

"And, Grampa, he says I can play in a game with the Stingrays," I said.

"This is good?" Max asked.

"You bet it's good," I said.

When we got to the beach, Max parked the car and we took out the fishing poles. Max led me across the sand to a long wooden pier stretching out into the ocean. The wood creaked when we walked on it, and when the waves rushed against the piles that held the pier up, it felt as if we were floating. It was still early, but there were ten other people fishing from the pier—I counted them—mostly old guys like Max. The tide was high. From the pier I could see the jetty where Candy's dog had fallen in. I tried not to think about it.

The sun hadn't risen very high, so Max took off his hat with the wide visor. He looked up at the sky. There wasn't a cloud in it.

"Duvid, I ordered a good day for us," he said. "How did I do?"

"You did great, Max."

We sat down near the edge of the pier. Max wouldn't let me sit on the edge with my legs dangling. He said it was because the fish would be scared off by the smell of my sneakers. But I knew he was afraid I might fall in.

I had only gone fishing once before, so Max baited my hook, and I dropped my line into the water. Then he dropped his line into the water without bait, without even a hook. Poor Max, I thought, he's getting senile.

"Max Levene," I said. "You don't even have a hook on your line."

"It's okay," he said. "I'm an old man. I don't need the excitement of catching a fish. Just sitting here by the ocean with my grandson on a beautiful day is enough."

"You're going to fish without a hook?"

"Yes. I tell you, when I was a boy I fished all the time. I caught such fish you wouldn't believe. One time I caught a fish that was bigger than our car; I swear to you, Duvid, this is true. But as I get older I don't like to see the fish struggle. Oh, I know, we need fish for food. Nobody enjoys a good halibut as much as your grampa, so I don't say we shouldn't fish. It's just not for me, anymore."

So we sat there for a long time, me with my hook in the water, and Max with his empty line. Not that it made any difference. The fish stayed away from both of us.

Finally Max said, "Duvid, I need from you a favor."

"Anything, Max. You want a tryout with the Celtics? I'll call K. C. Jones and set it up."

"We only have five days," he said. "I want you to help me find B.B."

"But, Max, everybody says it isn't B.B. who you saw."

"Everybody is *meshuggeneh*," Max said. "It was B.B. Believe your grandfather."

"Max, I don't know how to break this to you, but everybody thinks you're the one who's nuts."

"You think this?"

"No," I said. "I just think it was a man who looked like B.B."

"Okay," Max said, "then I'll make with you a deal. You don't have to help me find B.B. You will just help me find this man who looks like B.B. I will take it from there."

"You got a deal," I said, but I was really hoping Max would forget the whole thing. I didn't want to search for some guy who looked like B.B. I wanted to play basketball.

We sat quietly for a few minutes. Then Max got up and wandered over to the other side of the pier where some guy even older than Grampa was fishing all alone. Max was like that—he'd see a stranger he liked, and he'd just start talking to him as if the guy were his cousin or something. After ten minutes Max came back.

"Name's McGinnis," he said. "Used to be with Gillette in Somerville. Comes here every summer. Wife died about a year ago. Fixes lawn mowers, that sort of thing."

For a long time Max didn't say anything. I thought he must be thinking about Mr. McGinnis, but when he finally spoke, he said, "So, Duvid, last night your mother told you about the concentration camps?"

"Yes, but she didn't tell me what I really want to know."

"What do you want to know?"

"I want to know about you, Grampa. I want to know what happened."

Max looked at me carefully. "Are you sure you want to know this?"

Actually, I wasn't sure at all. The whole thing was making me kind of nervous. But I was sure that Max wanted to talk to somebody, and Max had always been there for me when I needed to talk. So I figured I owed him.

"Are *you* sure you want to tell this?" I asked.

Max edged closer, then snuck his hand into my belly, and tickled me gently the way he always did when I was little. "I'm sure if you're sure," he said.

"But, Duvid . . ." He held up one finger. "I warn you. This is not a bedtime story. You know what I'm talking?"

"Yeah, Grampa, I know what you're talking."

"Well, I was a young man once," Max said. "I know this is hard for you to believe."

"I know," I said. "A regular ice skater."

"Yes. A regular ice skater. Even after we had wives, B.B. and I would sometimes ice-skate. But I did not ice-skate so much after B.B. and Jacqueline went back to Heidelberg. They left because Jews were not treated so well in Vilna. To tell you the truth, they were not treated so well in Heidelberg either, but at least it was better, and it was home for B.B. In those days, Duvid, life was rough. There were many Jews in Vilna, and we lived in our own quarters. If a Jewish boy your age would go and walk around the city, the other boys would spit at him or chase him down the street like he was a dog. Sometimes they would beat him up. That's how it was. So we stayed with our own people in our own quarters.

"I remember my brother's bar mitzvah. It was in June 1941. I was thirty. He was the youngest. His name was Duvid, the same as you. You are named for my brother; did you know that?"

"Yes," I said. "Ma told me."

"Poor Duvid, he did not have such a great bar mitzvah."

"What do you mean?" I asked.

"Well, it was as if he had his bar mitzvah, but he didn't have it. You see, this was during the war . . .

shortly after the German soldiers had come in. We knew to keep our distance. If we would see a German soldier, quick, we would go inside, or we would climb up on a roof and hide until he was gone, or we would go over a fence and walk a long way around just to avoid him. So, a lot of people, they were afraid to go to *shul*. At Duvid's bar mitzvah, there were only a few. My father was there, my uncles, my other brothers. But not ten men. Not enough for the *minyan* to read from the Torah. So, my brother Duvid read the haftorah, and that was that. That was his bar mitzvah. Not like what you will have next year, with so many people there to celebrate such an important occasion."

"That's too bad," I said.

"Yes. That was. And there was much more that was bad. Very bad." Grampa paused, then smiled. "But soon after that my Klare became pregnant. Ah, but I told you this, already. These were not the best conditions to have a baby. Some of us decided then to go to America. We had relatives there. We would start a new life. First, my Klare and my sister, Malka, who was Klare's best friend, would go. And when they were safely gone, I was so happy, I danced in the street. Can you picture this, your grandfather dancing? Of course, I planned then to go myself with some others soon. But . . . it was not to be."

Grampa stared out at the waves. I waited.

"It was September. The Nazis suddenly marched into the old section, and they rounded up the people, thousands of them, like they were cows. And then . . ."

Grampa's eyes filled up, and I felt my heart thump inside my chest. "If you don't want to go on . . ."

He touched my shoulder, and said, "It's been a long time, my grandson, since I have talked about . . . these things. No, I will go on. You see, they took then my grandmother, my grandfather, my mother, my sisters, and my brother, Duvid. Klare's mother and sisters. Women and children, mostly. And just like that, they lined them up—thousands—and they shot them. They killed them. All of them. It was so horrible. And we stood there, helpless. We thought we would be next. But . . . next, what they did was they put up walls. Right in the middle of the street. They made the ghetto. And we became prisoners in our own quarters. German army cars were all over the place. Everywhere there were Nazi soldiers, always with the rifles and the steel helmets, and the swastikas around their arms. We could own nothing of value. That they took from us. We managed to hide some things in a hole somewhere, but, what good was that? We could go nowhere—there was a gate. And the Nazis would get drunk, and they would pound on the door and come into the house and take what they wanted. So we were left with very little.

"Those of us who were strong, like me, like my brothers—we worked on the railroad. They lined us up every morning, and took us to where we worked all day. Sometimes we would be away for weeks or

139

months at a time, working, repairing, building the railroad. If someone refused to work, they killed him. And if someone was too weak, or too sick, they shot him. They killed my father after a while because he was too weak. When I came back from the railroad one night, he was dead.

"One day in 1943 they burst into the ghetto, and quick, quick, they gathered all of us. Everyone. We took what we could with us, into a bag, but as I said, we had very little left anyway. They pushed us into the freight cars, and just when it seemed they could not fit in one more person, others would be forced inside. Hundreds of us, all pressed together in a single freight car. The doors were locked. It was dark, with only narrow slits between the wood to let in air. There was no room for anyone to sit down. We couldn't move. It was so uncomfortable, it was torture. There were no toilets. What could people do? They urinated, they vomited, they cried, they screamed. We were like this for days, cramped together, living in filth and terrible smells, and we had no food.

"When the doors finally opened, we prayed what awaited us would be better. It was not. The Nazis stood there. Soldiers with whips. There were beatings. Shootings. Families were separated. The women were sent in one direction, men in the other. In my line, we filed past a big man with a face I will never forget. This man smiled, and I thought, they will treat us better here. Ha! He looked at each Jew as he passed, and sent each one either to the left or the right. I was sent to the right. My brother Zalmon was sent to the right. Later I found out that the left means death, the right is life. And that same night I met a man who had come on a different train. He'd been at another camp, and he told me he had seen three Nazis tossing Jewish infants—babies—in the air, using them for targets. I could not believe this. In fact, I remember I called the man a liar. I did not believe that anyone, even a Nazi, could be that cruel. Now I know. There is nothing anyone could make up that is so horrible a Nazi would not do it.

"So, Duvid, I found out I was in Estonia. If you look on the map, you'll see it near the Gulf of Finland. In Narva.

"They took everything from us. Even my wedding ring. They shaved all the hair from our bodies. They tattooed numbers on our arms."

Max held out his arm and showed me the faded blue number on his forearm. I remembered being a kid and asking him about it, and he had told me it was his phone number in Germany. I had never really believed that, but I always knew I wasn't supposed to ask Max anymore about the tattoo.

"We were treated worse than animals," Max said. "They gave us one set of clothes, and that was it. And these clothes, Duvid, I wore all the time. Until it was all over. And it wasn't over for a long time.

"Again I worked on the railroad. And I worked on the lake, unloading cargo from the barges. Always there were soldiers nearby to whip you, to beat you, to kill you, if they did not like the way you worked. I once worked beside a boy, not much older than you.

He was a nice boy. But he broke his arm jumping on the barge. Then he could not lift the cargo. So, of course, they shot this boy. And they threw his body in the water.

"In the winter it was so cold, it was freezing. Sometimes it was thirty below zero, and still we worked. We slept on boards. We were cold, exhausted, and starving. But if we did not work, they would club us or kill us. So? What could we do? Talk back? They would kill us. Or worse, they would kill everybody in the unit. We got weaker and weaker. Sometimes we had only one potato that would have to last for two or three days. We would catch the rain in our hands to have something fresh to drink. We were skin and bones by now. In Vilna your grandfather was strong like an ox. But by this time I weighed maybe seventy pounds. That is less than you!

"But I still worked. Somehow I found the strength. I worked in shale mines, in coal mines, in quarries I worked. I worked in distilleries. But most of the time I worked on the railroad.

"People died around me all the time. They were barely more than skeletons. They dropped dead of exhaustion. They died of dysentery, malnutrition, typhoid. Why did I survive? I don't know. I had my brother. Much of the time we were together. And I had my Klare and my baby in my mind. While I worked I pretended I was with them. I imagined what the baby would look like, how I would bounce him on my lap. The baby was a boy in my mind mostly,

142

but sometimes I thought it would be nice to have a girl.

"One day at a time. This was the only way I could live. Each morning I vowed that I would get through the day and make the best of it. If I could help myself, or if I could help somebody else, I counted the day as a big success. If a Jew could go a whole day without a beating, this was a good day. If I could find a berry in the field and enjoy its sweetness, it was a good day. I thought, Max, maybe you will show them. They want you to die, but maybe you will be one of the ones who lives. I never stopped hoping that someday it would all be over.

"Anyway, I was sent from one concentration camp to another. In December of '44 I was sent on a boat to Danzig, in Germany. This was a concentration camp by the name of Stutthof. In Stutthof the Nazis killed thousands of Jews. As in other concentration camps, they were being sent to gas chambers. You know, the Nazis said that Jews—people like you and me, Duvid—were inferior, and we had to be exterminated. Monsters! They were monsters! But since I was still a good worker, they put me right to work. Again unloading barges. I remember there were lots of vegetables that time. Onions especially. I tell you, Duvid, to this day I do not eat onions."

Grampa took a deep breath. He waved his hand in the air, as though he were pushing away a swarm of bees.

"Well, then things changed. We knew something

143

was going to happen. The Americans, the Allies, they were coming. The planes were striking every day.

"So the Nazis marched us in the Black Forest. We walked and walked and walked—for a week we walked. If someone could not keep up, the Nazis clubbed him over the head, or shot him and left him there in a ditch. Zalmon and I were still together. But Zalmon was sick. I had to hold him up. I was so scared they would shoot him, too. How we managed, I don't know. I don't know.

"And then? Then one day it was morning, we were in the forest, somewhere in Württemberg, in Germany. Something felt different. It was quiet. And then we knew what it was. The guards were gone. They had disappeared, just like that. Gone. So everyone scattered. Zalmon and I walked until we came to a farm. A farmer gave us some soup, I remember—it was so delicious. And some warm bread. Ah. And a sugar beet. We spent the night, and the next day Zalmon already felt better. So we walked, and we came to the town of Salgau. I stayed there for a while until I could come back to my senses. We were free, but it took a long time to feel really safe. Finally, almost two years later, I was cleared to come to the United States, to Klare and my baby. Ellen, your mother. My brother Zalmon went to Israel. Then it was still Palestine. He died there, but he died free. My other brothers did not survive.

"And it was in Salgau that I met two men who knew B.B. and who told me he had died. They said his family—his mother, his father, his sisters and

144

brothers, all of them, had been shot or gassed or hung by the Nazis. Jacqueline, too. And she was not a Jew.

"It was all such a horrible nightmare. Too horrible to really happen. But you see, it did happen. And, Duvid, it must never happen again." He looked at me. "You are okay?"

I nodded. But I couldn't talk.

Grampa hugged me.

"You know, there is one thing I learned. I learned that from the moment I open my eyes in the morning, I must make the best of each day. Even if I wake up with an ache here or a pain there—and believe me, I wake up with a lot of aches and pains—at least, I am alive. And if I am going to be alive, I am going to live. And if I am on vacation I am going to enjoy it. And if I am with my wonderful grandson, fishing, and I don't like to catch the fish, then I should throw in a line without a hook, and just enjoy being with my grandson! Smell the fresh air. Listen to the sea gulls. You know what I'm talking?"

"Yeah, Grampa," I said through my tears. "I know what you're talking."

CHAPTER ELEVEN

Three Nazi soldiers came into my room. They had bayonets coming out of their hands, and they jabbed at me all over my body. I didn't bleed, but the bayonets stung. They made my whole body hot, and I kept shouting, "Cut it out! cut it out!" I was hysterical because I thought they were going to put me in a gas chamber. They dragged me out of bed and made me run down a long corridor that was like a basketball court, only it got narrower and narrower as I ran. The walls kept getting closer, and I knew they would crush me if I didn't get to the end, so I tried to run faster, but my legs felt slow and heavy, as if I were trying to run underwater. I was almost out of breath.

146

Finally I got to a door, and I ran into a room that had pieces of paper taped to all the walls. Each piece of paper had a list of names on it, and I ran from list to list, thinking that if I could find my name on one, the Nazis would go away. But there was only one name on this list, and it was written over and over. Nettie. Nettie, Nettie, Nettie, Nettie. It just went on and on. Then I felt a hand on my back, and it was Nettie. I could see her even though she was behind me. She was horrid-looking. Her face was scarred, and there were tiny little swastikas stitched into her forehead. "You're Jewish, too, you know," she said. Her face came closer. I started squirming, but I couldn't move. I was terrified. I expected the smell of gas. Then her face came down on mine, and I started gagging. I couldn't breathe. "Let me go!" I screamed, "let me go!"

"David," I heard someone call. "David, wake up. You're having a nightmare."

After I woke up I was still shaking and I was soaked with sweat. It was Nana. She held me for a long time the way she did when I was little and she used to baby-sit for me.

"What were you dreaming about?"

"The Holocaust," I said.

"I'm not surprised," she said. "Your grandfather told me you and he talked today."

When Nana said that, I laughed, the way you do sometimes when you're really scared. "He talked," I said. "I listened."

"Yes," she nodded. "Max, he is a talker."

"I'm sorry, Nana, did I wake you?"

"No," she said. "It's so hot, look at me, I'm *shvitzing*. Who can sleep?"

Nana was right. I had my window open, but the air in the room was hot and humid.

"So," she said. "The nightmare is all gone?"

"All gone," I said, but I still felt a little bit scared.

"Don't worry, it won't come back. It is always hard when you first learn about it."

"Nana," I said, "I don't think Grampa's crazy."

"Crazy? Who says my Max is crazy? Where do you get this idea?"

"I mean about seeing B.B. You and Ma and Dad act as if he's crazy when he says he saw B.B. But he can't be crazy. I mean if he went through all that Nazi stuff and didn't go crazy, then nothing could make him crazy. I don't think I could have survived like Grampa did."

"It's not that your Grampa's crazy," Nana said. "It's just that he's confused. It happens to men sometimes when they get old. To tell you the truth, it happens sometimes to women. Not to me, of course, but listen, there are some I could name. Like Sara Weinberg."

"Well, maybe Max is confused," I said, "but I'm not so sure. I'm going to help him find B.B. And if the guy we chased isn't B.B., I'm going to find him anyhow, and make him tell Grampa that he's not B.B. so Grampa won't have to wonder all the time."

"Is that what you want to do? You'll miss some of your basketball."

"That's okay," I said. "Max Levene is worth it."

"Grampa!" she said. "To *me* he is Max. To you he is Grampa!" She made a face, as if she were disgusted with me.

"Nana, you're a riot," I said, and I hugged her.

"This is funny, that you call your grandfather Max Levene?"

"No," I said. "What's funny is that you make such a big deal out of it after all these years. And I'll tell you something else: You're the best grandmother in the whole world even if you do drive me nuts sometimes."

Nana just beamed and tried to pretend she was tough. "Yes, yes, now don't be fresh. Go to sleep," she said, and she headed for the door. But on the way out she turned and said, "And, David, if you have another nightmare, you call your nana."

After Nana left, I was afraid to go back to sleep. For a long time I stayed awake, thinking about the horrible things that were done to Max. I wondered if anybody could ever make me do horrible things like that to other people. I tried to imagine myself killing Nazis, and it was easy. But I knew that was only make-believe. I don't think I could ever actually kill anybody.

In the morning I bicycled to Candy's house. She was getting ready to go roller-skating with her friends Emily and Anita, but when I told her I had decided I had to do something for Max Levene, she could see it was important to me, and she wanted to help. So she called up her friends and told them to go without her.

"The first thing we have to do is find Joe Ballantine and ask him if an old guy chased him down the street," I told her. "Maybe it was him, but maybe it wasn't."

We bicycled across the causeway to Newburyport.

The first place we looked was Market Square, where Max and I had sat the night we saw the painting. It seemed as if sooner or later everybody in Newburyport would walk by Market Square. Candy and I sat on a bench, feeding pigeons and watching people for a long time, thinking that any second we'd see those big bushy white eyebrows and we'd have our man. After a half hour or so we started taking turns going on reconnaissance missions. Candy would bicycle around the block a few times while I stood guard at Market Square. Then she would sit on the bench and keep guard while I bicycled around. Nothing.

It was a very hot morning, and I finally decided we should check out Annabelle's again. And while we were there I could buy Candy an ice-cream cone. That seemed like the least I could do.

While Candy ate her ice cream I talked to the same kid who had been there before. I asked him if he had seen the bushy-eyebrowed guy.

"He came in once," the kid said, smirking as if he were about to tell a joke. "But he didn't leave no business card."

We went to Fowles and stood by the stack of Racing Forms for a long time. I thought maybe the chief elf would arrange for Joe Ballantine to come in just when we happened to be there. I even said a prayer. But nothing happened. Finally I went back to the guy behind the counter, the fat guy who always had an unlit cigar in his mouth.

"Remember me?" I said.

"Yeah, you're the kid who was asking about Joe Ballantine."

"Right. How is old Joe? Seen him lately?"

"Sure. He comes in once or twice a week. I told him you were looking for him."

"Really?" I said. "You wouldn't happen to know where he lives."

"Got no idea, kid. Why don't you look in the phone book."

"Good idea!" I said. I had looked for Bernie Bauer in the phone book, but I had never looked for Joe Ballantine.

I went to the phone booth in front of Fowles and looked for Joe Ballantine's name in the phone book. It wasn't there. I walked back to Candy feeling disappointed, the way I felt when I couldn't find Bernie Bauer in the phone book, just before Nettie had attacked me.

Nettie!

That was it. Nettie. She would know where Joe Ballantine lived. I remembered what the kid at Annabelle's had said the first time I had questioned him. "She knows about everything and everybody." That's what he had said. Of course he had also said she was the meanest old lady in town, but I was trying to push

151

that from my mind. Nettie would know where Joe Ballantine lived; I was sure of it. Maybe if I called her up and asked her, she would tell me. She couldn't attack me over the phone.

"Candy," I called. I was excited. Candy was at the magazine stand, putting loose magazines back where they belonged. "What's Nettie's last name? I want to look up her phone number."

Candy laughed. "David, Nettie doesn't have a phone. She doesn't even have a house. She lives outside. She sleeps under porches or on benches in the park."

"Well, what does she do for money?"

"You ought to know. She crashes into people with her grocery cart and then tells them they have to give her money. She scares them so much, they give her a few bucks just to make her go away."

"Would she sell information?" I checked in my pocket to see if I had any money. I had five bucks that Nana had given me on my way out the door.

"Sure. She'd sell anything. Even things that aren't hers."

"We have to talk to her," I said.

"Correction, David. *You* have to talk to her. Nettie and I are not on speaking terms, mainly because she's nuts. People say she's got a dagger in her shopping bag."

"I thought you said that was just a story."

"Yes, but what if it's a *true* story?"

"Okay," I said. "You don't have to talk to her. But help me find her."

We made a list of all the places where Candy had seen Nettie over the years. There was the sidewalk in front of a drugstore where Nettie sometimes stood throwing stones at teenagers. There was the parking lot where she had practically killed me with her grocery cart. There was a coffee shop where Nettie liked to tell people sad stories about her past so they would feel sorry for her and buy her coffee and doughnuts. There were three other places. We each took a list of places and rode off on our bicycles to see if we could find her. If I found Nettie, I was supposed to ask her where Joe Ballantine lived. If Candy found Nettie, she was supposed to find me and tell me where the old hag was.

When I found the drugstore Candy had told me about, I parked my bicycle about a hundred yards from the entrance. If Nettie was in the doorway, I didn't want to get pelted with stones. There was a row of cars parked along the street all the way to the drugstore and past it. I sneaked around behind the cars. I crouched down low, and as I moved closer to the front of the store I listened for her awful screech. Finally I got behind the car that was directly in front of the entrance to the drugstore. I lifted my head slowly and peeked. There were two customers coming out of the store, but no sign of Nettie. I sighed with relief.

Suddenly I felt a hand on my shoulder.

"Yipes!" I shrieked. The people coming out of the store stared at me. I swung around.

"David, it's me." It was Candy. "Did I scare you?"

"No," I said, trying to regain my composure. "I shriek a lot. It's good for the lungs."

"I found Nettie," Candy said. "She's at the coffee shop."

The coffee shop was on State Street, near the library, but Candy led me the long way around so that when we came around the corner of High Street we could look down the hill toward the coffee shop. Nettie was out on the sidewalk with her shopping cart. Even though it was a boiling hot day she was wearing a gray raggedy overcoat. She was muttering, and scowling at the air. She held her hand out in front of her, as if she expected people to drop money into it. Every time somebody went by without dropping a coin into her hand Nettie waved a fist at them and screamed something. I couldn't hear what she was saying, but it sounded as if she were putting a curse on them.

"I feel like a jerk," Candy said.

"Why?"

"I just feel like a lousy friend because I'm afraid to go down there with you and talk to the old monster."

"Hey! No problem! It's okay to be afraid," I said. "I've been afraid lots of times."

"Really?" Candy said. "You don't mind if I chicken out?"

"No," I said. "Do you want to go home?"

"No. I'll wait here. You're sure it's okay?"

"Sure," I said.

"You're great," she said. "You're really great."

154

And then, "Promise me you'll be careful. Maybe Nettie really does have a dagger."

"I'll be careful. I promise."

I started rolling down the hill toward Nettie. I didn't pedal. In fact, I held the brakes. No sense rushing into things. Suddenly, there she was, standing in front of the coffee shop looking like the creature from beyond.

The memory of my dream came back to me. The Nazis. The bayonets. The walls closing in on me. Nettie's awful face smothering me. I pulled my bike over to the sidewalk and parked it against the library, thinking I would walk the rest of the way. As I got closer I began to think, this is pointless; she probably doesn't even know Joe Ballantine. And even if she does, she probably wouldn't tell me where he lives. Maybe she would take my money and lie. Besides, she could attack me again with her shopping cart. She could throw things at me. And what about the dagger? I could get killed.

I got about thirty feet from Nettie, and I stopped. I could see those cold blue eyes staring at me. It was as if I had come to a wall and could not take another step. I was petrified. I didn't want to face Nettie alone. Max, I thought. Sure, Max would come with me. Yeah, me and Max Levene, we'd grill the old lady good until she told us everything she knew; then we'd find Joe Ballantine and we'd get the truth out of him. I turned around and walked back to my bicycle.

"Did you see it, David?" Candy said when I got back to the top of the hill. "Did you see the dagger?"

"I'm not sure," I said. "There could have been something poking out of her coat. I figure it will be safer if I get Max Levene and we go back together."

Candy could see that I was scared, but we didn't talk about it on the way back to Plum Island.

I still felt pretty much like the wimp of the year when we got to Candy's house. I told her I was going back with Max right away. We got off our bikes and stood in front of her cottage.

"You're sure you don't want me to come?" she said.

"Nah," I said. "This is something Max and I have to do alone. But thanks for helping me and everything."

When I got home, I rushed up on the porch.

"Max Levene," I said. "Calling Max Levene."

My mother was at the screen door even before I got to it. "David," she said, "Max is in the hospital."

"The hospital? What happened?"

"They're not sure," Ma said. "They think it was a heart attack."

"A heart attack?" I felt a chill run through me.

"Not a severe one," Ma said. "They're not sure. Grampa felt weak, and he was out of breath, so Nana and I took him to the hospital in Newburyport. He's okay, David."

"I want to go to see him."

"Not now. Visiting hours are four to six. Later we'll bring him his things, and you can see him before he leaves."

"Leaves for where?"

"Home," Ma said. "He won't be coming back to the cottage. Your father will come up and drive Grampa and Nana back to Newton. Grampa will be more comfortable there, and he'll have his own doctor, just in case."

"I've got to go," I said.

"I told you, visiting hours aren't until four."

"Not the hospital," I said. "I've got to find Joe Ballantine before it's too late. If Grampa leaves, we'll probably never see Ballantine again."

Ma must have thought I was nuts.

I climbed back on my bike and pedaled like a madman over the bridge back to Newburyport. I knew it was my fault that Max had the heart attack. I shouldn't have asked him about the Holocaust. That's what had done it, I was sure. Now I had to find B.B. for Max, or at least show him that it was Joe Ballantine, not B.B.

By the time I got back to State Street I was exhausted from pedaling. I saw Nettie. She was right in front of the coffee shop, getting ready to leave. She turned and began pushing her grocery cart down the hill. I went down the hill after her.

"Nettie!" I hollered when I was almost caught up with her. She turned around and snarled at me like a scruffy old alley cat. I pulled up in front of her, but I didn't get off my bike. My heart was beating fast, but I didn't know if it was from the bicycling or the fear of Nettie.

"What do you want?" she screeched.

She put her hand to her collar. For an instant I

157

thought she was getting ready to pull out the dagger. Then I realized she was putting a hand up to protect herself. I had come bicycling at her suddenly, screaming her name, and she was as frightened of me as I was of her.

"I have to talk to you," I said.

"What about?" she said suspiciously.

"Joe Ballantine. Do you know who he is?"

"Of course I know who he is. Do you think I'm a fool?"

"Where does he live?"

Nettie leaned forward and peered at me, as if she were looking through a hole in a wooden fence.

"Why should I tell you?" she said.

"Because," I said.

"Because what?" she said.

I glanced at the coffee shop behind her. "Because I'm going to buy you lunch," I blurted out. Oh, David, I thought, now you've done it.

Nettie looked at me suspiciously for a few seconds. "All right," she screeched, "but I'm warning you. Don't try to walk out without paying for my lunch." She parked her grocery cart on the sidewalk, and I parked my bicycle right behind it.

I led Nettie to a booth way down back. The waitress came, and Nettie ordered a cup of coffee and a chicken salad sandwich. "On toast," she hollered at the waitress, "and I want that toast well-done, or I'm not paying for it. I want it dark, real dark."

Nettie looked at me after the waitress was gone. "You can't trust anybody these days," she said. "You

158

tell them dark toast, and they give you pumpernickel. You can't trust anybody."

"Joe Ballantine," I reminded her.

"What about him?"

"Anything. What do you know about him?"

"He's an artist," she said.

"An artist?" I couldn't believe it.

"Teaches over at the community college where all those snotty kids go. Plays the horses. No wonder he never has any money. If he didn't play the horses, maybe he'd have a few dollars sometimes for a person down on her luck."

"Where does he live?"

"Plum Island," she said.

"Plum Island. Whereabouts?"

"How would I know? I don't have no fancy car to go driving around Plum Island with. Why don't you ask Hooley Fuller?"

Hooley Fuller. I recognized the name. He was the artist who had painted the lobster picture, the one with the bee.

"Hooley Fuller knows Joe Ballantine?"

"Of course they know each other. I just said so, didn't I?"

"How?"

"How what?"

"How do they know each other?"

"Hooley was a student of Ballantine's. The two of them are thick as thieves. If you ask me, I've got no use for either one of them. Never give me a dime, neither one of them. Not a dime."

159

"Where does Hooley live?"

"I need a cigarette. You don't smoke, do you, kid?"

"No."

She glanced at the cigarette machine. "Maybe if you gave me some money for cigarettes, I could remember where Hooley lives."

I pulled the five-dollar bill out of my pocket and dropped it on the table. Nettie snatched it up, as if I were going to take it back. She went to the counter, and I heard her shouting, "Change, I need some change here." She got cigarettes out of the machine and came back to the table. Already she was smoking.

"Boardman Street," she said, blowing smoke in my face.

"What number?"

"How would I know?" she said. "I don't frequent that part of town. Too much riffraff. It's fifty something. Brown house. Got a big stained-glass window over the porch. That window would fetch a pretty penny, believe you me."

I knew Boardman Street. I had gone down it on my bicycle.

"Thanks," I said. I stood up and rushed for the door.

"Hey, wait a minute," Nettie shouted, "you got to pay for my lunch."

"Take it out of the five dollars," I said.

As I was getting on my bicycle I could see Nettie through the window, chasing me. When she got to the door, I was pedaling away. "Your house will burn for this," she screamed. "Rats will eat your feet."

I was halfway to Boardman Street when I realized what I had done. I had faced Nettie. I had talked to her. And I had lived.

My head was spinning with what I had found out. Joe Ballantine was an artist. He knew Hooley Fuller. This was incredible. I felt like a master detective. I had discovered a link between the lobster painting and the man with the bushy eyebrows. It had to be B.B. Otherwise it would be too much of a coincidence.

Hooley Fuller's house wasn't hard to find. There was only one stained-glass window on the street. I climbed the front steps and rang the doorbell. I didn't want to take any chance on losing Joe Ballantine, so I had decided to fib a little.

A tall young guy came to the door. He had long black hair down to his shoulders, and he wasn't wearing any shirt, just a pair of white pants that were covered with every color of paint you can imagine. He didn't say hello or anything. He just looked at me and waited for me to speak.

"Are you Hooley?" I said.

"Yes."

"My name is David Newman," I said. "I'm looking to take art lessons."

"I don't give art lessons," he said. "Where did you get my name?"

"At the gallery," I said. "I'm a great admirer of your work. They told me you didn't give lessons, but they said you took lessons from a guy name Joe Ballantine."

161

"Yes," he said. "Joe is a great artist and a great teacher."

"Well, I thought if I could take lessons from him, well . . . well, maybe someday I'd be as good as you."

Hooley's face lit up. "You really know my work?" he said.

"Oh, sure. My favorite is the still life, the one with the lobster."

"Thanks," he said. "Nice to meet a kid who appreciates art. Too bad you're not old enough to buy it. Come on in, kid. I'll show you where Joe lives."

Hooley took me into his studio. The smell of paint and turpentine filled the air, and there was junk all over the place, and paintings and brushes and rolls of canvas. All of the paintings had the bee in the lower right-hand corner.

Hooley ripped a big sheet of paper off a thick pad and put it on the floor. Then he took a brush that already had green paint on it, and he drew a map to Joe's house on Plum Island.

"He'll be home," Hooley said. "The track is closed today."

"Thanks," I said. "Before I leave I have a question. How come you sign your paintings with a bee?"

Hooley smiled. "I got that from Joe," he said. "He taught me everything I know, so it's my way of showing respect for him."

"Joe Ballantine signs with a bee?"

"He signs with two bees. I sign with one. He's the master. I'm the student."

"I see," I said, and I tried not to show how excited I was.

By the time I got to Joe Ballantine's house on the beach, I was a nervous wreck. I couldn't believe it. Grampa had been right all the time. Bushy Eyebrows *was* B.B. And he lived just six blocks from our cottage. I had really done something important for Max Levene.

Ballantine's house was a small cottage near the ocean. There were hundreds of flowers in front of the house and a long path between them with little white wire fences on either side. I left my bicycle out on the sidewalk and started slowly up the path, but before I even got to knock, the door swung open, and there he was. Joe Ballantine. B.B. Bushy Eyebrows. He smelled of paint, just like Hooley, and I could see bits of it on his fingernails, but his clothes weren't all messy. He wore white pants, and a long-sleeve shirt, the same as he had the day we chased him down State Street.

"What do you want?" he asked.

He was trying to sound mean, but his voice came out soft. Sort of like Max's.

"My name's David Newman," I said. "I want to talk to you."

"You're the kid who was with that crazy old man who chased me last week."

"He's not crazy," I said. "He's my grandfather. I'm sorry if he scared you, but he thinks you're an old friend of his."

163

"Well, I'm not."

"May I come in?"

He stared at me for a while; then his look softened and he stepped aside, signaling for me to come into the house.

The room I stepped into was the living room. It was dark and cool. Off to the right was an open wooden stairway leading up to a loft filled with sunlight—probably where he painted.

Ballantine walked through the room and into a small kitchen.

"You want some lemonade?" he asked. "It's hot out there."

"Yes, thanks."

He came back into the room and handed me a glass of lemonade. "Have a seat," he said. He glanced across the room suddenly, as if he had seen something.

"So your grandfather thinks he knows me, huh?"

"Yes," I told him. "He says you're B.B. Bernie Bauer. He used to know you in Poland years ago. And Germany."

While I was talking Ballantine walked casually across the room and took a small framed picture from the wall. I thought it was something he wanted to show me, but all he did was open a desk drawer and shove the picture inside.

"So tell me," he said, "what does your grandfather say about this Bernie Bauer fellow? Am I supposed to owe him money or something?"

"No. He says you were friends. Good friends. He says he knew your wife, Jacqueline."

"Well, he's wrong," Ballantine said coldly. "He must be thinking of someone else."

"No," I said. Suddenly I was shouting. "Max Levene you don't fool. Grampa's right. You are B.B. I know it. Why don't you admit it?"

"Don't be ridiculous, kid. Don't you think I know who I am? My name's Joe Ballantine."

"No, it's not. It's Bernie Bauer. I know. Because you sign your paintings with the bees. Just like B.B."

"The bees? Is that what this is all about?" He put his hand to his jaw and rubbed it the way some people do when they're thinking. "Bauer, Bauer? Yes, it was Bauer. You're right. Must have been your grandfather's friend."

"What are you talking about?" I said.

"I'll explain . . ." he said. He went into the kitchen and poured himself a glass of lemonade. He came back slowly.

"When I was a young man, I went to live in France," he said. "That's what all young artists do, if they can. I guess I thought it would make me a great artist just to breathe the air of Paris. While I was there I toured all over Europe. When I was in Germany, in Heidelberg, I came upon several paintings by the same man. I'd forgotten his name until you just reminded me of it. Bernie Bauer. All of the paintings were signed with the double bee. I liked the work a lot. I was young and impressionable, so I took the signature of the bees as my own, because it fit my name. My name is Benjamin, really. Such a name! So everybody called me Joe for my middle name, Joseph. But it's really Benjamin Ballantine. Two B's, just like your grandfather's friend."

"You're not B.B.?" Now I was totally confused.

"No. Of course not. That's what I've been telling you."

I looked into his face. His eyes seemed so friendly. It was hard to believe he might be lying to me.

"You don't believe me, do you?" he said.

"Yes," I said. "I mean, I don't know. I mean, Max swears it was you."

"I understand," he said. "Look, I'm an old man myself. Sometimes I think I see people from the past. It's one of the hazards of growing old."

"All right," I said, "let's say you're not B.B."

"I'm not, kid; I told you that."

"Okay, you're not. Just do me a favor. Come and see Max and let him see that you're not B.B. Then he'll be okay."

"Can't do that," he said. "I'm a busy man. I've got work to do. I've already interrupted my work to talk to you."

"But you have to," I said. I was pleading. "Max is in the hospital."

"Hospital?"

"They think he had a heart attack."

"Is he all right?" Ballantine said.

"They think he'll be okay. But they want to send him home. He'll be leaving Newburyport tonight.

166

And if you don't come to the hospital and let him see that you're not B.B., he'll spend the rest of his life thinking that he saw B.B. and that B.B. ran away from him."

"You'd better go now," Ballantine said.

"Huh?"

"You'd better leave. I've got work to do."

"Will you come to the hospital? Will you talk to Max?"

"No. Of course not," he said. "You're calling me a liar. Why don't you just go back and tell your grandfather what I've told you. My name is Joe Ballantine, not Bernie Bauer."

"But you have to come!" I shouted. "Don't you understand? It's important to my grampa. It's my chance to do something for him."

"Don't shout at me, kid. I don't owe you any explanations. I don't have to prove anything to you or your grandfather. Now get out."

I wanted to scream some more, call him names, do something. I didn't understand why he was being so mean. All I wanted was to help Grampa. But his eyes had gone hard on me, and I knew that I couldn't force him.

"Okay," I said. "I'm going." I walked to the door. He followed me.

"Look," I said. "I'm sorry I shouted. It's just that I'm upset about Grampa being sick and all. No hard feelings?" I put out my hand for him to shake.

"No hard feelings, kid." He smiled and gave me his hand.

167

This was it, I thought. I hoped I had the right hand. I held his hand as tight as I could so he couldn't pull it away. Then I reached over and tried to unbutton his cuff.

"Hey, what the hell are you doing?" he said.

"I have to know," I said, "I have to know."

I couldn't get the button undone. He started to yank his arm. I held on tight. I grabbed the cuff of his sleeve.

"Are you crazy?" he shouted. He took his other hand and started pushing my head. I held on to the arm, but I could feel it getting away. I ripped open the cuff, and I heard the sleeve tear as I pulled it back.

It was there. I only saw it for an instant before he yanked his hand out of mine, but I had seen it, I was sure. On his forearm. The faded blue tattoo. His concentration camp number.

"Get the hell out of here!" he screamed. "Don't ever come back, or I'll have you arrested!"

I ran out the door and got on my bicycle.

CHAPTER TWELVE

Later we all met in Max's hospital room. Everybody was there. My mother and father. Nana. Candy. Max was sitting up on his bed. He was dressed, and he had his suitcase on the floor beside him. He looked pretty good, but the doctors wanted him to go to a bigger hospital in Newton for a couple of days. Then he could go home and rest.

Everybody just stood around listening while I told Max about my visit to B.B. Candy couldn't believe B.B. lived so near to her. After I finished telling my story, everybody congratulated me, as if I were a detective or something.

"So when are we going back?" I said to Max.

"What'cha talkin', going back?"

"To B.B.'s," I said. "To talk to him."

"What for?"

"What do you mean, what for? We know it's him. I proved it, with the number on his arm and the bees and everything. That story he told me about seeing the paintings in Germany is a lie."

Max looked at me. Then he looked at everybody else.

"Would you excuse me while I talk to my grandson?" he asked. Everybody filed out.

When we were alone, Max patted a spot beside him on the bed. "Duvid, sit," he said.

I sat on the bed. "Why do you want to go back?" Max said. "This man threw you out of his house. If I were you, I would not take that as an invitation to return."

"We've got the goods on him, Grampa."

"Goods? What is goods?"

"It means we know it's him. We've got proof. If he sees you face-to-face, he can't deny he's B.B."

"Duvid, maybe the others, they are not so sure that this man is B.B. But you and I, we know. That's because we're smart. Max Levene and David Newman you don't fool. Am I right?"

"You're right," I said.

"So why would we go back?"

"To make him admit it," I said.

"But if we know it is B.B., why would we need to make him admit it?"

"I don't know, Grampa. I just know we shouldn't

let him get away with this. I hate him for what he's doing. He's supposed to be your friend, and he won't even talk to you."

Max didn't say anything for a while. He had that faraway look he sometimes got when he was thinking about the old days.

"B.B. was a good man," he finally said. "And the Nazis got him. I don't know what he went through. But I tell you this—if B.B. does not want to speak to me, he must have a very good reason. We must respect that. We don't go back."

"But, Grampa, I wanted to do something for you."

"You've done plenty, believe me. If you want to do me a favor, next time you see B.B. you tell him Max Levene forgives him."

"I won't be seeing him again," I said.

"Oh?"

"I'm going back with you," I said.

"Why would you do this?" Max said. He looked at me suspiciously.

"To look out for you. You're going to be in the hospital for a couple of days. You'll need someone to talk to and bring you books. And we can play chess, the way we used to when I was a kid. And you'll need me to smuggle in food. If you think they're going to feed you bagels and cream cheese in the hospital, you're crazy, Max Levene. Besides, it's my fault you had the heart attack."

"Oh?" Max said. "You have this power, to reach inside of a man's heart, so it should attack him?"

171

"Well, no. But I made you talk about the Nazis and all that. That's why you had the heart attack."

"Hmmn. The doctors don't know why I would have a heart attack, but a boy of twelve, he knows. Very odd. Duvid, there is no saying why a person has a heart attack. But let's pretend you are right. I was talking about the Holocaust because of seeing B.B. So perhaps we should blame him for the heart attack."

"I guess so, but—"

"Better still," Max said, "we should blame the Nazis. Without them, I would have no Holocaust to talk about."

"Well, sure, it's their fault, but—"

"The Nazis were about forty years ago. Now let me see, how old were you forty years ago?"

"Grampa! I wasn't even born."

"Hmmn. Then I guess you had nothing to do with my heart attack."

"Max Levene, you're trying to confuse me."

"Duvid, listen to me. You cannot take the blame for everything that happens near you. Sometimes things happen and they are not your fault. You know what I'm talking?"

"Yeah, I know what you're talking."

Max put his arm around me.

"But I'm going back with you, anyhow," I said.

"What about this besketball you wanted to play with the Stingers?"

"*Basketball*, Max, basketball. And it's Stingrays, not Stingers. That's not important. You're important. Besides, Larry Cataldo taught me a lot of new things I can use when I get home. See, I thought I was left off the team just because I was short. But it wasn't just that. There was a lot of stuff I didn't know about basketball, but I know it now. Anyhow, I talked to my friend Randy last night, and we came up with this great plan—a basketball league for short kids. We're going to call it the Shrimp League. I'm anxious to get to work on it."

"Okay," Max said. "You've convinced me. You come back with me. You'll play chess with an old man in the hospital: You'll have a great time. Now go and say good-bye to your little girlfriend, Kendy."

"She's not my girlfriend, Max."

"Whatever," he said. "Now go."

When I got out in the hall, I told everybody that I was going to stay with Nana for a couple of days so I could visit Max in the hospital. Everybody just smiled as if I had done something wonderful. Ma decided she might as well pack up and go home, too. I asked Candy to go for a walk so we could say good-bye.

We walked down a long corridor without saying anything until we came to a door and walked out onto the lawn in front of the hospital.

"I'm sorry I'm leaving so suddenly and all," I said.

"That's okay. I understand," Candy said. "I think it's great that you love Max so much."

We walked along the lawn.

"David, will you write to me?"

"Sure," I said.

"Great. Tell me everything. Tell me about what Max is up to, and about basketball and school and your girlfriends."

I asked Candy to thank Larry Cataldo for me. Then we walked back up to Max's room so my mother could drive Candy home. We hugged, and the last thing I said to Candy was "I hope that someday you get to live in a big mansion on High Street."

CHAPTER THIRTEEN

Max Levene was dead. It was still so hard to believe. All the time the rabbi was talking I had hardly heard a word because I was thinking about Max and that vacation on Plum Island the previous summer.

"David, it's time to go," I heard my mother say. I looked up, startled. The rabbi had stopped talking, and all the people were standing and working their way toward the door so they could go to the cemetery.

I spun around quickly, looking for the face, the bushy eyebrows, the silvery white hair. B.B. was gone.

I pushed my way into the line of people. "Excuse me," "excuse me," I said again and again, as I squeezed myself through the crowd to get to the front as quickly as possible. I had to catch him. When I got to the front door of the funeral home, I looked around, expecting to see him driving away.

But there he was. He had just walked a short distance from the chapel, and now he was standing on the sidewalk, as if he were waiting for me.

I walked slowly toward him, not knowing what I would say.

When I got close to him, he smiled at me weakly. He had a large manila envelope in his hand.

"You have no right to be here," I shouted at him. "You have no right."

"I came to pay my respects to Max," he said.

"Your respects. Who cares about your respects? You were cruel to my grandfather. You ran away from him. You knew it was Max, and you ran away, and he never knew why."

"Yes. I knew it was Max," he said. "That's why I ran away."

He started walking slowly along the sidewalk. He seemed to know that I would stay with him, even though I had to go to the cemetery. Far behind us I could hear the sounds of people coming out of the funeral home and getting into their cars. I walked along. I wanted to hurt B.B. somehow, call him names, punish him for what he had done, tell him how sad he had made Max.

But all I could say was "How could you do that to Max? He was your friend."

"Yes, he was. Maybe the best friend I ever had," B.B. said.

We came to a small park, and B.B. sat down under a tree. "Sit with me for a few minutes. I'll try to explain."

I sat in the grass under the tree and looked into his face. His eyes were sad, the way Max's sometimes got.

"David," he said, "did your grandfather ever tell you about the war, about what the Nazis did to the Jews?"

"I know about the Holocaust," I said. "He thought that you died."

"I did," B.B. said. He stared at the ground. When he looked up, I could see that there were tears in his eyes.

"I was in a concentration camp in Germany. I don't have to tell you what went on. I'm sure Max told you enough. The Nazis killed my Jacqueline. They had already killed my mother, my father, my brothers. And friends, dozens of friends. Somehow I had survived all that. But when they killed my Jacqueline, they killed me, too.

"When it was over, I was still breathing. I could walk. But I was dead. I knew that the only way I could live was to be born again as someone else. I came to America. I took the name Ballantine. For forty years I did not talk about the war and what went on. I did not see anybody from my childhood. I did not go back to Germany. I could not—would not—allow myself

177

even to think about all those people who were killed. I kept only one thing from the past. . . ."

He handed the envelope to me. "And now I give it to you," he said. I looked at him to see if he expected me to open it in front of him. He didn't seem to care.

"When I saw Max that day, I was terrified," he said. "To talk to him would be like ripping open my heart and seeing all the things I did not want to think about. Do you understand? I am not a brave man. I could not let that happen. Your grandfather, he was brave. He did not put the past out of his mind. He lived with it. But, please, David, don't hate me because my way of dealing with it was different. A person does what he can."

He put his head down, and I knew he was crying.

"But the memories came to me anyhow. Since the day you came to see me, I could not put the past out of my mind. I have talked to a lot of people about the things that happened. I cry a lot. But I'm getting stronger. I will be okay. I wanted to see Max, but I did not know where he was."

"How did you know he died?"

"A girl came to my house and told me. She said she was a friend of yours, and you had told her about Max."

"Candy," I said.

B.B. reached out and put a hand on my shoulder. "I am sorry," he said. "I am truly sorry that Max had to die wondering whether or not I was B.B."

"He didn't wonder," I said. "He knew. Max Levene you don't fool."

B.B. was really sobbing now, and he seemed embarrassed about it. I guess I was embarrassed, too, not about his crying, but about the fact that just moments ago I had been so angry with him. He stood up. "Anyhow, I know this is a hard time for you. I just wanted to give you the envelope and try to explain. I hope you understand."

"I think I do," I said.

This time B.B. didn't offer his hand. I guess he was afraid I'd attack him again. He just managed as much of a smile as he could through his tears, and he walked away.

"Hey, B.B.," I called.

He turned around.

"Max Levene told me once I should do him a favor. He said the next time I see you I should forgive you for him."

"So?" B.B. said.

"So, you're forgiven."

B.B. waved good-bye, turned, and walked away. "Say hello to Candy," I shouted, but I don't know if he heard me.

It was time to go to the cemetery. I just wanted another minute alone. I went back and sat under the tree and opened the envelope. As soon as I opened it, I knew what was inside. It was the framed picture that B.B. had taken down from the wall in his living room on the day I was at his house.

I pulled it out. It was a newspaper picture of two boys holding a trophy in their hands. The caption was in German, but it wasn't hard to figure out that these kids had won some kind of ice-skating award. One kid had big bushy eyebrows. Obviously, it was B.B. The other kid looked familiar. He looked a lot like the face I had seen in the mirror when I had gone into the men's room to cry about Max Levene. It was Max, smiling proudly at his ice-skating trophy. And he looked like me. A regular David Newman he was.